Better Homes and Gardens®

PASTA

© Copyright 1983 by Meredith Corporation, Des Moines, Iowa.
All Rights Reserved. Printed in the United States of America.
First Edition. Fourth Printing, 1984.
Library of Congress Catalog Card Number: 82-80529
ISBN: 0-696-00855-6 (hard cover)
ISBN: 0-696-00857-2 (trade paperback)

On the cover:
Marinated Tomatoes with Pasta (see recipe, page 68)

BETTER HOMES AND GARDENS® BOOKS
Editor: Gerald M. Knox
Art Director: Ernest Shelton
Managing Editor: David A. Kirchner

Food and Nutrition Editor: Doris Eby
Department Head–Cook Books: Sharyl Heiken
Senior Food Editors: Rosemary C. Hutchinson, Elizabeth Woolever
Senior Associate Food Editor: Sandra Granseth
Associate Food Editors: Jill Burmeister, Julia Malloy, Linda Miller,
    Alethea Sparks, Marcia Stanley, Diane Yanney
Recipe Development Editor: Marion Viall
Test Kitchen Director: Sharon Stilwell
Test Kitchen Home Economists: Jean Brekke, Kay Cargill,
    Marilyn Cornelius, Maryellyn Krantz, Marge Steenson

Associate Art Directors (Creative): Linda Ford, Neoma Alt West
Associate Art Director (Managing): Randall Yontz
Copy and Production Editors: Marsha Jahns, Nancy Nowiszewski,
    Mary Helen Schiltz, David A. Walsh
Assistant Art Directors: Harijs Priekulis, Tom Wegner
Graphic Designers: Mike Burns, Trish Church-Podlasek, Alisann Dixon,
    Mike Eagleton, Lynda Haupert, Deb Miner, Lyne Neymeyer,
    Stan Sams, D. Greg Thompson, Darla Whipple, Paul Zimmerman

Editor in Chief: Neil Kuehnl
Group Editorial Services Director: Duane L. Gregg

General Manager: Fred Stines
Director of Publishing: Robert B. Nelson
Director of Retail Marketing: Jamie Martin
Director of Direct Marketing: Arthur Heydendael

Pasta
Editors: Linda Miller, Marcia Stanley
Copy and Production Editor: Mary Helen Schiltz
Graphic Designer: Faith Berven

Our seal assures you that every recipe in *Pasta* has been tested in the Better Homes and Gardens Test Kitchen. This means that each recipe is practical and reliable, and meets our high standards of taste appeal.

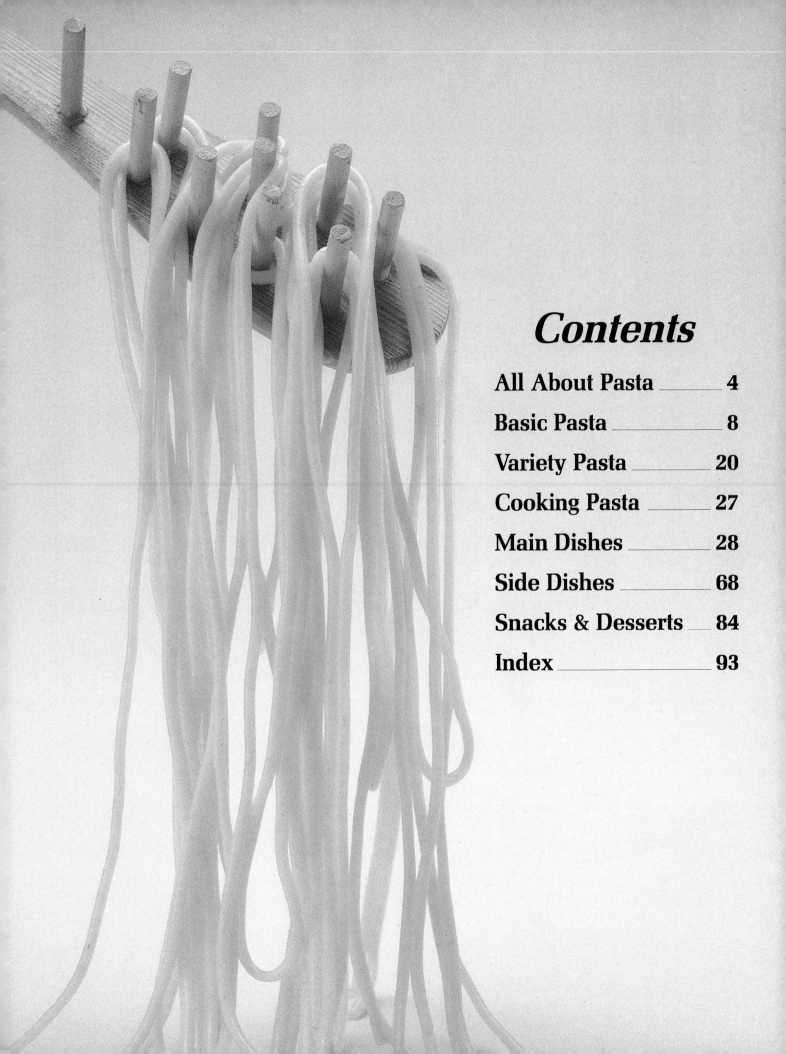

Contents

All About Pasta

Derived from what is basically a flour and water mixture, pasta has long been associated primarily with Italian cuisine. This relationship probably began when Marco Polo introduced Italy to the noodle after his trip to China in the 1270 s. However, there is evidence that ravioli was being eaten in Italy 20 years prior to Polo's travels.

Today, we are recognizing pasta's international appeal. The Germans delight in their spaetzle, the Chinese enjoy their wontons and eggrolls, and the Japanese savor their soba noodle. In this book, we focus on the many varieties of pasta there are to choose from and the variety of ways to use each pasta as an entrée, an accompaniment, a dessert, and a snack. The photos on the following pages will help you identify your pasta choices; the rest of the book will help you create something delicious.

Elbow Macaroni

Alphabets

Conchiglie

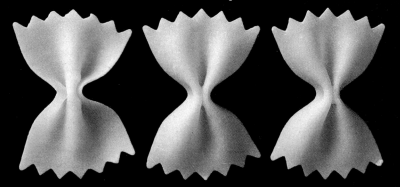
Farfalle

Orzo or Rosamarina

Rotelle

Cavatelli

Rigatoni

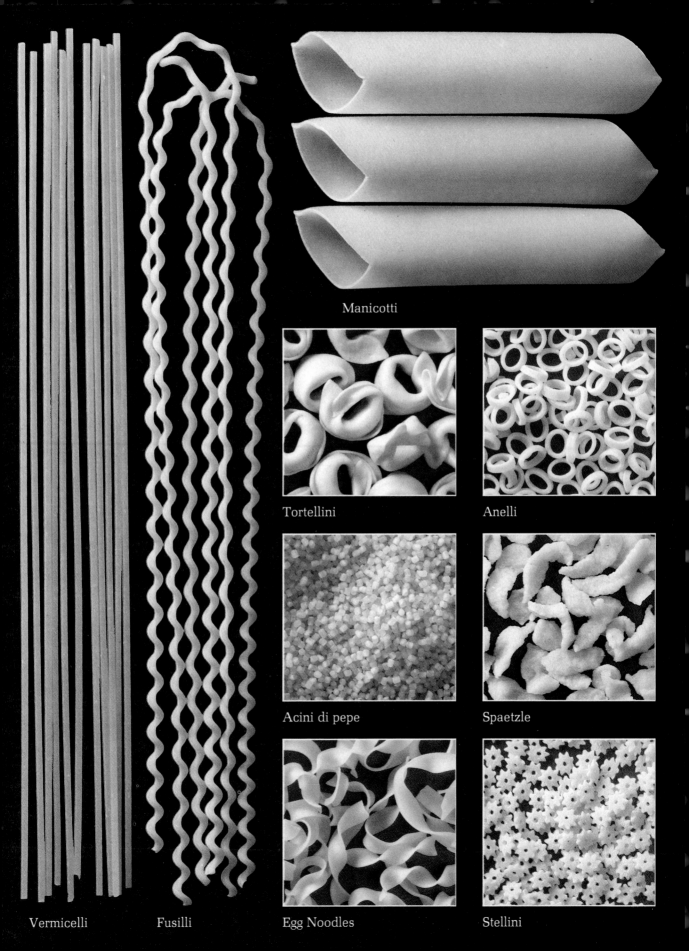

Vermicelli

Fusilli

Manicotti

Tortellini

Anelli

Acini di pepe

Spaetzle

Egg Noodles

Stellini

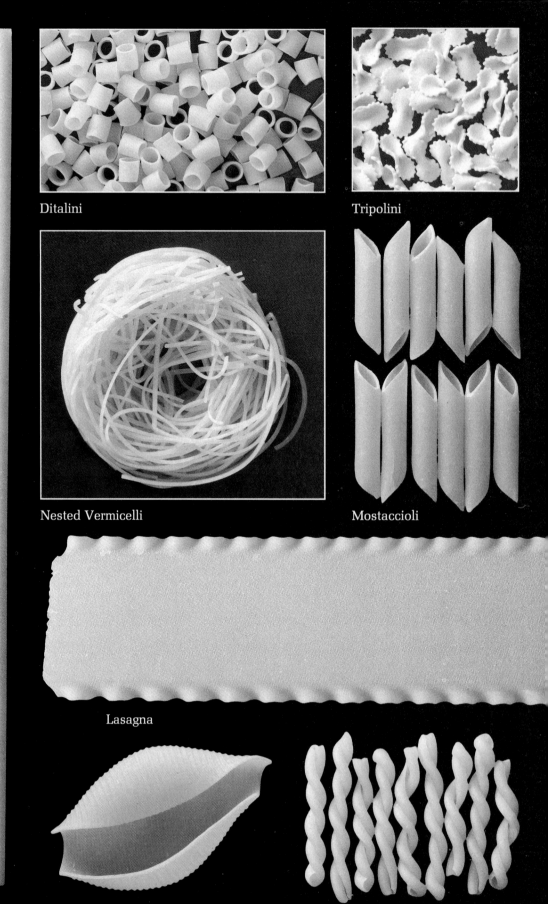

Ditalini

Tripolini

Nested Vermicelli

Mostaccioli

Lasagna

Ziti

Conchiglioni

Gemelli

Ravioli

Couscous

Rice Sticks

Ruote

Fettuccine

Mafalda

Egg Roll Wrapper

BASIC PASTA

2⅓ cups all-purpose flour
½ teaspoon salt
2 beaten eggs
⅓ cup water
1 teaspoon olive oil
   or cooking oil

In a large mixing bowl stir together *2 cups* of the flour and salt. Push the mixture against the edge of the bowl, making a well in the center. In a small mixing bowl, combine eggs, water, and olive oil or cooking oil. Stir egg mixture into the flour-salt mixture all at once, mixing till the dry and liquid ingredients are well combined.

Sprinkle the kneading surface with the remaining ⅓ cup flour. Turn dough out onto the floured surface. Knead till the dough is smooth and elastic (8 to 10 minutes). Cover and let rest 10 minutes.

Divide dough into thirds or fourths. On a lightly floured surface roll each third of dough into a 16x12-inch rectangle or each fourth of dough into a 12-inch square. If using a pasta machine, pass dough through the machine till ¹⁄₁₆ inch thick. Dust with additional flour, as necessary, to prevent sticking. Cut and shape as desired. Cook according to the directions on page 27. Makes 1 pound fresh pasta.

In preparing a recipe that does not use the entire amount of pasta dough, store the remaining dough in the refrigerator for up to 3 days or freeze it for longer storage.

In a large mixing bowl stir together *2 cups* of the all-purpose flour and the salt. Push the flour-salt mixture against the edge of the bowl, making a well in the center. Use a wooden spoon for this step.

In a small bowl combine the eggs, water, and oil. Add this mixture to the flour and salt all at once, pouring it into the well. Mix with a wooden spoon till the dry and liquid ingredients are well combined.

The olive oil or cooking oil in the dough adds tenderness to the finished pasta product.

Sprinkle kneading surface with remaining ⅓ cup flour. Knead till smooth and elastic.

For ease in kneading, curve fingers over dough, pull toward you, then push down and away with heel of your hand. Give a quarter-turn; fold toward you, and push down again.

Shape dough into a smooth ball. Cover dough with a towel to help prevent a dried-out surface. Let rest 10 minutes. This allows the dough to relax and makes it easier to roll.

If you stop to rest or are interrupted during the kneading process, be sure to cover dough.

To roll out dough using a rolling pin, divide into three or four portions. On a floured surface roll each third into a 16x12-inch rectangle or each fourth into a 12-inch square. If dough becomes too elastic during rolling, cover and let rest.

To roll out dough using a pasta machine, divide into thirds or fourths. Pass dough through machine at widest opening. Continue resetting and rolling dough through machine at narrower openings, repeating till about 1/16 inch thick.

9

WONTON SKINS

2 cups all-purpose flour
½ teaspoon salt
½ cup warm water
  Cornstarch

In a mixing bowl stir together the flour and salt. Slowly stir in the warm water to make a stiff dough. Turn the dough out onto a lightly floured surface and knead for 10 to 15 minutes or till the dough is smooth and elastic. Cover and let rest for 20 minutes.

Divide dough into fourths. Roll each fourth into a 12-inch square. Keep remaining dough covered. For wontons, with a sharp knife or a pastry cutter, cut the dough into 3-inch squares. To prevent the squares from sticking together, sprinkle with a little cornstarch; stack and refrigerate the skins in a plastic bag. Fill according to directions on these pages; cook as directed in individual recipes. Makes 64 wonton skins.

Egg Roll Wrappers: For egg roll wrappers, prepare the Wonton Skins dough as directed above; roll each fourth into a 12-inch square. With a sharp knife or a pastry cutter, cut the dough into 6-inch squares. Sprinkle the squares with a little cornstarch to prevent them from sticking together; stack and refrigerate the wrappers in a plastic bag. Fill and cook the egg rolls according to the directions in individual recipes. Makes 16 egg roll wrappers.

Sprinkle a little cornstarch over the wonton squares to prevent them from sticking to one another during storage. Stack and refrigerate the wonton skins in a plastic bag. Brush off any excess cornstarch before using the skins.

To make wontons, position a wonton skin with one point toward you. Spoon desired filling just below center of skin, in corner facing you. In most recipes, about 2 teaspoons filling is used for each wonton. This may vary slightly, however, so check individual recipes before filling.

When choosing a filling for your wontons, keep in mind that it should contain ingredients that can be chopped finely so they fold up easily into the skin.

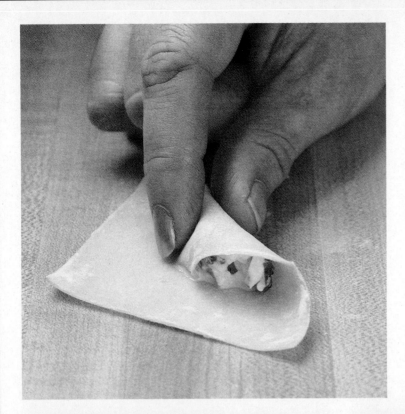

Fold bottom point of the wonton skin over the filling; tuck the point under the filling. Roll once toward the center, covering the filling as shown, and leaving about 1 inch unrolled at the top of the skin.

Moisten the right-hand corner of the filled skin with water. Grasp the right- and left-hand corners of skin as shown; bring these corners toward you, below the filling, till they meet.

Moistening with water helps make a tight seal, ensuring that no filling will escape.

Overlap the left-hand corner over the right-hand corner; press the ends together to seal them securely.

If preparation time is limited, buy packages of fresh or frozen wonton skins at an Oriental market or large supermarket.

11

SPAETZLE

2 cups all-purpose flour
1 teaspoon salt
2 beaten eggs
¾ cup milk
   Buttered bread crumbs (optional)

In a mixing bowl stir together flour and salt; make a well in the center. In a glass measure combine eggs and milk. Stir into the flour-salt mixture all at once, pouring into the well. Mix till the dry and liquid ingredients are well combined.

Bring a kettle of salted water to boiling. Pour spaetzle batter into a colander with large holes (at least ³⁄₁₆-inch in diameter) or spaetzle maker. Hold colander or spaetzle maker over kettle. Press batter through colander or spaetzle maker so it falls in droplets into the boiling water to form the spaetzle. (If batter is too thick to push through, thin it with a little milk.)

Cook and stir about 5 minutes. Remove cooked spaetzle with a slotted spoon. Drain well. Sprinkle spaetzle with buttered bread crumbs, if desired. Or, cook as directed in recipe. Makes 4 cups.

In a mixing bowl stir together the flour and salt. Gently push mixture against the edge of the bowl, making a well in the center. Combine eggs and milk. Add to the flour-salt mixture all at once, pouring it into the well. Mix till ingredients are well combined.

Bring a kettle of salted water to boiling. Pour the spaetzle batter into a colander with large holes or into a spaetzle maker. Hold colander or spaetzle maker over the kettle of boiling water. Press the batter through the holes in the colander or spaetzle maker so it falls in droplets into the water. If the batter is too thick to push through, thin it with a little milk. Cook and stir about 5 minutes. Drain.

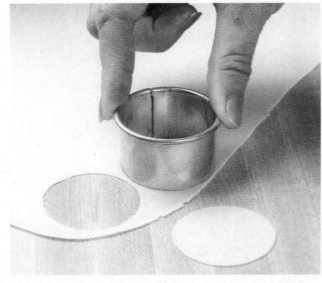

To cut desired pasta dough into tortellini, roll out dough by hand or with a pasta machine. With a 1½-inch round cutter, cut dough into circles. Cut out as many circles from rolled dough as possible. Gather up any scraps and cover them, then reroll with remaining dough.

Using the filling of your choice, fill the tortellini by placing ¼ teaspoon filling in the center of each circle. To seal in the filling, fold the circle of dough in half to make a half-moon. Moistening the dough with water if necessary, press edges of the dough together with your finger.

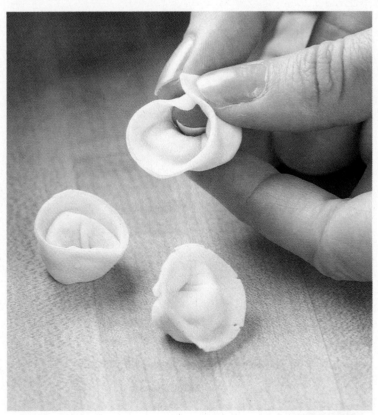

To shape tortellini, place index finger against fold; bend tortellini around your finger, bringing the outer two corners together. Press one corner over the other, moistening if necessary. Pinch the ends firmly together to secure the tortellini. Lay the filled tortellini on a floured surface. Let dry for a few minutes before cooking.

When preparing any of the filled pastas, fill and shape them immediately after rolling out and cutting the dough. Otherwise, the dried-out dough is difficult to shape.

To cut pasta dough into ravioli, roll out dough by hand or with a pasta machine. Use a sharp knife to cut the pasta into 2-inch-wide strips. Leaving a ½-inch margin around the edges, place about 1 teaspoon desired filling at 1-inch intervals on one strip of the dough.

Using a pastry brush or your finger, moisten the dough with water around the mounds of filling. Lay a second strip of dough atop the first.

Using the side of your hand, press the pasta around each mound of filling so that the two moistened strips of dough stick together. With a fluted pastry wheel or a sharp knife, cut the pasta between the mounds of filling to separate into uniformly sized individual ravioli.

To prevent the filled ravioli (or any of the other filled pastas) from tearing or sticking together till you are ready to cook them, place them, well separated, on a floured surface.

Another way to make ravioli is to roll the dough into 2 portions. Roll ravioli rolling pin over one portion. Dot with filling between markings. Top with second portion.

Line up ravioli rolling pin with mounds of filling. Roll pin across top, pressing to seal. Or, using a ravioli stamp, press down between mounds to seal and cut the ravioli.

After rolling pin across top, use a fluted pastry wheel or a sharp knife to cut along the indentations between the rows of filling to separate the squares into individual ravioli.

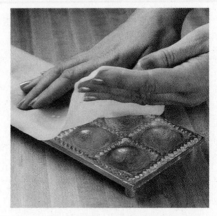

A third way to make ravioli is to lightly flour the hollows of a ravioli frame. Place a strip of pasta dough over the frame, being sure that the dough completely covers the frame. Lightly press dough into the hollows of the frame with your fingers. Fill the hollows with the desired filling.

Top with another strip of pasta dough that completely covers the frame. Roll a standard rolling pin over the top, pressing firmly so the ravioli are sealed and scored. Trim excess dough.

Invert frame carefully onto a floured surface to remove the ravioli. (Tap one end of the frame on the surface, if necessary, to remove ravioli from frame.) Using a sharp knife, cut squares into individual ravioli.

Linguine

To cut pasta dough into linguine, roll out dough by hand or with a pasta machine. After rolling, let stand about 20 minutes to dry surface slightly. To cut by hand, roll up dough loosely. Cut into ⅛-inch-wide slices. Lift; shake to separate.

To cut linguine using a pasta machine, pass dough through an ⅛-inch-wide cutting blade. Support the pasta dough entering the machine with your free hand, if necessary. Cut with a knife into desired lengths.

Lasagna

To cut pasta dough into lasagna noodles, roll out the dough by hand or with a pasta machine. Using a sharp knife, cut the dough into 2½-inch-wide strips. Or, for decorative edges, cut the dough into strips with a fluted pastry wheel. Use a knife to cut the strips into the desired lengths.

Farfalle

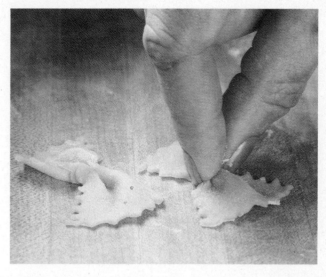

To cut the pasta dough into farfalle, roll out the dough by hand or with a pasta machine. Using a sharp knife or, for decorative edges, a fluted pastry wheel, cut the dough into rectangles about 2 inches long and 1 inch wide.

To form into a butterfly shape, pinch together the center of each rectangle.

Gather up any scraps of dough and cover them so they can be rerolled with any remaining dough.

Fettuccine

To cut pasta dough into fettuccine, roll out by hand or with a pasta machine. After rolling, let dough stand about 20 minutes to dry surface slightly.

To cut by hand, roll up dough loosely. Cut into ¼-inch-wide slices; lift and shake to separate. To cut using a pasta machine, pass dough through a ¼-inch-wide cutting blade. Cut into desired lengths.

Noodles: To make noodles, cut dough ¼-inch-wide as directed above. Cut into 2-inch lengths.

Manicotti

To cut pasta dough into manicotti, roll out by hand or with a pasta machine. Using a sharp knife, cut dough into rectangles about 4 inches long and 3 inches wide. Cook manicotti according to directions on page 27, or fill and cook at a later stage as directed in individual recipes.

To fill manicotti, place the pasta rectangle with one point toward you. Using the filling of your choice, fill the manicotti by spooning 2 to 3 tablespoons of filling onto the rectangle. Spread the filling diagonally across and just below the center of the rectangle.

To shape, begin at the bottom point of the pasta rectangle and roll the pasta around the desired filling.

Cannelloni are cut the same size as manicotti and can often be substituted for manicotti. To fill cannelloni, place the cooked rectangle with the short side toward you. Spoon about 2 tablespoons of filling across and just below the center. Beginning at the bottom edge, roll the pasta around the filling.

Filled Stars

To cut pasta dough for filled stars, roll out dough by hand or with pasta machine. Using a sharp knife or, for decorative edges, a fluted pastry wheel, cut dough into 3-inch squares. Using the filling of your choice, place about 1 tablespoon of filling in center of each square.

After cutting the dough into squares and filling with about 1 tablespoon of desired filling, use a pastry brush or your finger to brush the edges of the squares with water. Moistening with water helps make a tight seal, ensuring that no filling will escape.

To form the cut dough into a starlike shape, join two opposite corners of each square over the filling; pinch together. Then fold the other two corners into the center and pinch closed. Pinch the cut edges together to enclose the filling securely.

Roll-Ups: To make roll-ups, cut the dough into 3-inch squares as directed above for Filled Stars. Position a square with one point toward you. Roll up the dough jelly-roll style. Press end to seal.

Variety Pasta

CARROT PASTA

- 1 16-ounce can diced carrots, well drained
- 2 eggs
- 3¾ cups all-purpose flour
- ½ teaspoon salt
- 1 teaspoon olive oil *or* cooking oil

Place carrots and eggs in a blender container; cover and blend till pureed.

In a mixing bowl stir together *3¼ cups* of the flour and salt. Make a well in the center. Add the carrot mixture and the olive oil or cooking oil. Mix well.

Sprinkle the kneading surface with the remaining ½ cup flour. Turn dough out onto the floured surface. Knead till the dough is smooth and elastic (8 to 10 minutes). Cover and let rest 10 minutes.

Divide dough into thirds or fourths. On a lightly floured surface roll each third of dough into a 16x12-inch rectangle or each fourth of dough into a 12-inch square. If using a pasta machine, pass dough through machine till ⅟₁₆ inch thick. Dust with additional flour, as necessary, to prevent sticking. Cut and shape as desired. Cook as directed on page 27. Makes 1¾ pounds fresh pasta.

WHOLE WHEAT PASTA

- 2⅓ cups whole wheat flour
- ½ teaspoon salt
- 2 beaten eggs
- ⅓ cup water
- 1 teaspoon olive oil *or* cooking oil

In a mixing bowl stir together *2 cups* of the flour and salt. Combine eggs, water, and olive oil; add to flour. Mix well.

Sprinkle the kneading surface with the remaining ⅓ cup flour. Turn dough out onto the floured surface. Knead till the dough is smooth and elastic (8 to 10 minutes). Cover; let rest 10 minutes.

Divide dough into thirds or fourths. On a lightly floured surface roll each third of dough into a 16x12-inch rectangle or each fourth into a 12-inch square. If using a pasta machine, pass dough through machine till 1/16 inch thick. Dust with additional flour as necessary. Cut and shape as desired. Cook as directed on page 27. Makes 1 pound fresh pasta.

After kneading, the gluten in flour is so elastic that the dough snaps back if rolled out immediately. A resting period relaxes the gluten.

SPINACH PASTA

- 2¾ cups all-purpose flour
- ½ teaspoon salt
- 2 beaten eggs
- ¼ cup very finely chopped cooked spinach, well drained
- ¼ cup water
- 1 teaspoon olive oil *or* cooking oil

In a mixing bowl stir together *2¼ cups* of the flour and salt. Make a well in the center. Combine eggs, spinach, water, and olive oil; add to flour. Mix well.

Sprinkle the kneading surface with the remaining ½ cup flour. Turn the dough out onto floured surface. Knead till the dough is smooth and elastic (8 to 10 minutes). Cover and let rest 10 minutes.

Divide the dough into thirds or fourths. On a lightly floured surface roll each third of dough into a 16x12-inch rectangle or each fourth of dough into a 12-inch square. If using a pasta machine, pass dough through machine till 1/16 inch thick. Dust with additional flour, as necessary, to prevent sticking. Cut and shape as desired. Cook as directed on page 27. Makes 1¼ pounds fresh pasta.

HERB PASTA

2⅓ cups all-purpose flour
1 teaspoon dried basil, crushed, *or*
   dried marjoram, crushed, *or*
   dried sage, crushed
½ teaspoon salt
2 beaten eggs
⅓ cup water
1 teaspoon olive oil *or* cooking oil

In a mixing bowl stir together *2 cups* of the flour, herb, and salt. Combine eggs, water, and olive oil or cooking oil; add to flour. Mix well.

Sprinkle kneading surface with the remaining ⅓ cup flour. Turn dough out onto floured surface. Knead till smooth and elastic (8 to 10 minutes). Cover and let rest 10 minutes.

Divide dough into thirds or fourths. On a lightly floured surface roll each third of dough into a 16x12-inch rectangle or each fourth of dough into a 12-inch square. If using a pasta machine, pass dough through machine till ¹⁄₁₆ inch thick. Dust with additional flour, as necessary, to prevent sticking. Cut and shape as desired. Cook as directed on page 27. Makes 1 pound fresh pasta.

Pasta machines are designed to simplify the task of rolling out and cutting pasta dough. Start by dividing the dough into thirds or fourths. Pass dough through widest roller opening. Repeat at same setting if necessary. If the dough becomes sticky, lightly dust with flour. Set machine at next narrower opening and pass the dough through the machine, repeating till smooth. Continue resetting machine at narrower openings and rolling to about ¹⁄₁₆-inch thickness. If dough tears, fold it over and reroll. If dough looks stretched, fold over and reset to a wider opening.

VARIETY PASTA

When looking for olive oil, the best places to shop are Italian grocery stores or gourmet shops. The finest olive oils are "first pressings." Look for bottles labeled as such.
After opening, store olive oil in a cool, dark place, but not in a refrigerator. Once opened, oil may become rancid in hot weather, so check the oil frequently. Unopened olive oil keeps for up to 12 months.

CORN PASTA

1⅓ cups all-purpose flour
1 cup Masa Harina tortilla flour
½ teaspoon salt
2 beaten eggs
⅓ cup water
1 teaspoon olive oil *or* cooking oil

Stir together *1 cup* of the all-purpose flour, the tortilla flour, and salt. Combine eggs, water, and olive oil; add to flour. Mix well.

Sprinkle kneading surface with the remaining ⅓ cup all-purpose flour. Turn dough out onto floured surface. Knead till smooth and elastic (8 to 10 minutes). Cover and let rest 10 minutes.

Divide dough into thirds or fourths. On lightly floured surface roll each third into a 16x12-inch rectangle or each fourth into a 12-inch square. If using a pasta machine, pass dough through machine till ¹⁄₁₆ inch thick. Dust with additional flour as necessary. Cut and shape as desired. Cook as directed on page 27. Makes 1 pound fresh pasta.

SESAME PASTA

2⅓ cups all-purpose flour
¼ cup sesame seed, toasted
½ teaspoon salt
2 beaten eggs
⅓ cup water
1 teaspoon sesame oil, olive oil, *or* cooking oil

Stir together *2 cups* of the flour, sesame seed, and salt. Combine eggs, water, and sesame oil; add to flour. Mix well.

Sprinkle kneading surface with the remaining ⅓ cup flour. Turn dough out onto floured surface. Knead till smooth (8 to 10 minutes). Cover; rest 10 minutes.

Divide dough into thirds or fourths. On lightly floured surface roll each third into a 16x12-inch rectangle or each fourth into a 12-inch square. If using a pasta machine, pass dough through machine till ¹⁄₁₆ inch thick. Dust with additional flour as necessary. Cut and shape as desired. Cook as directed on page 27. Makes 1 pound fresh pasta.

ONION PASTA

1 tablespoon minced dried onion
⅓ cup water
2⅓ cups all-purpose flour
2 beaten eggs
1 teaspoon olive oil *or* cooking oil

To soften minced dried onion, combine it with water. In a mixing bowl place *2 cups* of the flour. Combine eggs, olive oil, and onion-water mixture; add to flour. Mix well.

Sprinkle kneading surface with the remaining ⅓ cup flour. Turn dough out onto floured surface. Knead till smooth and elastic (8 to 10 minutes). Cover and let rest 10 minutes.

Divide dough into thirds or fourths. On lightly floured surface roll each third of dough into a 16x12-inch rectangle or each fourth into a 12-inch square. If using a pasta machine, pass dough through machine till 1/16 inch thick. Dust with additional flour as necessary. Cut and shape as desired. Cook as directed on page 27. Makes 1 pound fresh pasta.

PASTA DIABLE

2⅓ cups all-purpose flour
1 tablespoon chili powder
½ teaspoon salt
2 beaten eggs
⅓ cup water
1 teaspoon olive oil *or* cooking oil

Stir together *2 cups* of the flour, chili powder, and salt. Combine eggs, water, and olive oil; add to flour. Mix well.

Sprinkle kneading surface with the remaining ⅓ cup flour. Turn dough out onto floured surface. Knead till smooth and elastic (8 to 10 minutes). Cover and let rest 10 minutes.

Divide dough into thirds or fourths. On lightly floured surface roll each third of dough into a 16x12-inch rectangle or each fourth into a 12-inch square. If using a pasta machine, pass dough through machine till 1/16 inch thick. Dust with additional flour as necessary. Cut and shape as desired. Cook as directed on page 27. Makes 1 pound fresh pasta.

23

PARSLEY PASTA

2⅓ cups all-purpose flour
1½ cups snipped fresh parsley
½ teaspoon salt
2 beaten eggs
3 tablespoons water
1 teaspoon olive oil *or* cooking oil

In a mixing bowl stir together *2 cups* of the flour, parsley, and salt. Combine eggs, water, and olive oil or cooking oil; add to flour. Mix well.

Sprinkle kneading surface with the remaining ⅓ cup flour. Turn dough out onto floured surface. Knead till smooth (8 to 10 minutes). Cover; rest 10 minutes.

Divide dough into thirds or fourths. On lightly floured surface roll each third of dough into a 16x12-inch rectangle or each fourth into a 12-inch square. If using a pasta machine, pass dough through machine till 1/16 inch thick. Dust with additional flour, as necessary, to prevent sticking. Cut and shape as desired. Cook as directed on page 27. Makes 1 pound fresh pasta.

To store unstuffed pasta, cut and spread out on a pasta drying rack, or improvise by making your own drying rack out of a coat hanger and draping the pasta over it. Let stand overnight or till completely dry. Wrap in clear plastic wrap or foil or place in an airtight container. Store in dry place. For freezer storage, cut pasta; let dry at least 1 hour. Wrap it in moisture-vaporproof wrap; freeze up to 8 months. To store stuffed pasta, fill and shape as desired. Dust lightly with flour; let dry for 1 hour. For use within 2 days, refrigerate in a covered container. For longer storage, wrap it in moisture-vaporproof wrap and freeze up to 8 months.

TOMATO PASTA

2¾ cups all-purpose flour
½ teaspoon salt
2 beaten eggs
1 6-ounce can tomato paste
1 teaspoon olive oil *or* cooking oil

In a mixing bowl stir together *2¼ cups* of the flour and salt. Combine the eggs, tomato paste, and olive oil or cooking oil; add to flour. Mix well.

Sprinkle kneading surface with the remaining ½ cup flour. Turn dough out onto floured surface. Knead till smooth and elastic (8 to 10 minutes). Cover and let rest 10 minutes.

Divide dough into thirds or fourths. On lightly floured surface roll each third of dough into a 16x12-inch rectangle or each fourth of dough into a 12-inch square. If using a pasta machine, pass dough through machine till ¹⁄₁₆ inch thick. Dust with additional flour, as necessary, to prevent sticking. Cut and shape as desired. Cook as directed on page 27. Makes 1¾ pounds fresh pasta.

Pasta has long had the reputation of being a fattening food. The truth is the calories lurk in those rich cheese and tomato sauces that smother pasta dishes. One-half cup cooked noodles averages only about 100 calories. Although it is not generally recognized for its nutritional contributions, pasta adds protein, carbohydrates, and vitamins to our diets. Packaged pasta products are usually enriched further with thiamine, riboflavin, niacin, and iron.

BEET PASTA

1 16-ounce can diced beets, well drained
2 eggs
3¾ cups all-purpose flour
½ teaspoon salt
1 teaspoon olive oil *or* cooking oil

Place beets and eggs in a blender container; cover and blend till pureed.

Stir together *3¼ cups* of the flour and salt. Stir in beet mixture and olive oil; mix well.

Sprinkle kneading surface with the remaining ½ cup flour. Turn dough out onto floured surface. Knead till smooth (8 to 10 minutes). Cover; rest 10 minutes.

Divide the dough into thirds or fourths. On lightly floured surface roll each third of dough into a 16x12-inch rectangle or each fourth into a 12-inch square. If using a pasta machine, pass dough through machine till ¹⁄₁₆ inch thick. Dust with additional flour as necessary. Cut and shape as desired. Cook as directed on page 27. Makes 1¾ pounds fresh pasta.

ORANGE PASTA

3⅓ cups all-purpose flour
½ teaspoon finely shredded orange peel
2 beaten eggs
1 6-ounce can frozen orange juice concentrate, thawed
1 teaspoon olive oil *or* cooking oil

Stir together *3 cups* of the flour and orange peel. Combine eggs, concentrate, and olive oil; add to flour. Mix well.

Sprinkle kneading surface with the remaining ⅓ cup flour. Turn dough out onto floured surface. Knead till smooth (8 to 10 minutes). Cover; rest 10 minutes.

Divide dough into thirds or fourths. On lightly floured surface roll each third of dough into a 16x12-inch rectangle or each fourth into a 12-inch square. If using a pasta machine, pass dough through machine till ¹⁄₁₆ inch thick. Dust with additional flour as necessary. Cut and shape as desired. Cook as directed on page 27. Makes 1½ pounds fresh pasta.

LEMON PASTA

3⅓ cups all-purpose flour
½ teaspoon salt
2 beaten eggs
1 6-ounce can frozen lemonade concentrate, thawed
1 teaspoon olive oil *or* cooking oil

In a mixing bowl stir together *3 cups* of the flour and salt. Combine eggs, lemonade concentrate, and olive oil or cooking oil; add to flour. Mix well.

Sprinkle kneading surface with the remaining ⅓ cup flour. Turn dough out onto floured surface. Knead till smooth and elastic (8 to 10 minutes). Cover and let rest 10 minutes.

Divide dough into thirds or fourths. On lightly floured surface roll each third of dough into a 16x12-inch rectangle or each fourth of dough into a 12-inch square. If using a pasta machine, pass dough through machine till ⅟₁₆ inch thick. Dust with additional flour, as necessary, to prevent sticking. Cut and shape as desired. Cook as directed on page 27. Makes 1½ pounds fresh pasta.

Even though it is best to serve pasta immediately after cooking, this may not always be possible. If dinner is a little late, here are a couple of ways to hold the cooked pasta till you are ready to serve it. Transfer pasta to a colander; cover and place the colander atop a pot of hot water. The steam keeps the pasta warm. Or, drain the pasta and return it to the empty pot. Place the covered pot in a warm oven for a short time. In both methods, tossing the pasta with a little oil or butter prevents it from sticking.

PINEAPPLE PASTA

3⅓ cups all-purpose flour
½ teaspoon salt
2 beaten eggs
1 6-ounce can frozen pineapple juice concentrate, thawed
1 teaspoon olive oil *or* cooking oil

In a mixing bowl stir together *3 cups* of the flour and salt. Combine eggs, pineapple juice concentrate, and olive oil or cooking oil; add to flour. Mix well.

Sprinkle kneading surface with the remaining ⅓ cup flour. Turn dough out onto floured surface. Knead till smooth and elastic (8 to 10 minutes). Cover and let rest 10 minutes.

Divide the dough into thirds or fourths. On a lightly floured surface roll each third of dough into a 16x12-inch rectangle or each fourth of dough into a 12-inch square. If using a pasta machine, pass the dough through the machine till dough is ⅟₁₆ inch thick. Dust with additional flour, as necessary, to prevent sticking. Cut and shape as desired. Cook as directed on page 27. Makes 1½ pounds fresh pasta.

The capabilities of electric pasta machines vary. Some machines mix, knead, cut, and extrude the pasta dough, while others require you to mix the dough by hand and then place it in the machine for kneading, cutting, and extrusion. Machines vary also in the number and the type of attachments that accompany them.

Before preparing any of the recipes in this book in an electric pasta machine, check the manufacturer's instructions carefully.

*Green Noodles
With Meatballs*

Cooking Pasta

COOKING DIRECTIONS

3 quarts water
1 tablespoon salt
1 tablespoon cooking oil (optional)
8 ounces pasta

In a large kettle or Dutch oven bring water and salt to a rolling boil. If desired, add oil to help keep large pasta separated. When the water boils vigorously, add pasta a little at a time, so water does not stop boiling. (Hold long pasta, such as spaghetti, at one end and dip the other end into the water. As the pasta softens, gently curl it around in the pan till immersed.) Reduce the heat slightly and continue boiling, uncovered, till the pasta is tender but still slightly firm, a stage the Italians call *al dente* (to the tooth). Refer to the approximate cooking times given below. Stir occasionally to prevent the pasta from sticking. Taste often near the end of the cooking time to test for doneness.

When the pasta tests done, immediately drain it in a colander. Transfer the cooked pasta to a warm serving dish. Serve immediately. (If necessary to hold the pasta for a short time, drain and return to the empty cooking pan, add 2 to 3 tablespoons butter to prevent the pasta from sticking, then cover pan to keep the pasta warm.) Makes about 4 cups cooked pasta.

COOKING TIMES

Pasta	Cooking Time
Homemade Pasta (fresh)	
Cannelloni	2 to 3 minutes
Cappelletti	10 minutes
Farfalle	1½ to 2 minutes
Fettuccine	1½ to 2 minutes
Filled Stars	8 to 10 minutes
Lasagna	2 to 3 minutes
Linguine	1½ to 2 minutes
Manicotti	2 to 3 minutes
Noodles	1½ to 2 minutes
Ravioli	6 to 8 minutes
Tortellini	10 minutes

Cook frozen or dried homemade pasta a few minutes longer than fresh pasta.

Pasta	Cooking Time
Packaged Pasta	
Acini di pepe	5 to 6 minutes
Alphabets	4 to 5 minutes
Anelli	9 to 10 minutes
Cavatelli	12 minutes
Conchiglie	15 minutes
Conchigliette	8 to 9 minutes
Conchiglioni	23 to 25 minutes

Pasta	Cooking Time
Packaged Pasta (continued)	
Ditalini	8 to 9 minutes
Farfalle	10 minutes
Fettuccine	10 to 12 minutes
Fusilli	15 minutes
Gemelli	10 minutes
Lasagna	10 to 12 minutes
Linguine	8 to 10 minutes
Macaroni (elbow)	10 minutes
Mafalda	10 to 12 minutes
Manicotti	18 minutes
Mostaccioli	14 minutes
Noodles	6 to 8 minutes
Orzo or Rosamarina	5 to 8 minutes
Rigatoni	15 minutes
Rotelle	8 to 10 minutes
Ruote	12 minutes
Spaetzle	12 minutes
Spaghetti	10 to 12 minutes
Stellini	5 to 6 minutes
Tripolini	5 to 6 minutes
Vermicelli	5 to 6 minutes
Ziti	14 minutes

GREEN NOODLES WITH MEATBALLS

Pictured on page 26—

- 1 beaten egg
- ⅓ cup milk
- ¾ cup soft bread crumbs
- 2 tablespoons grated Parmesan cheese
- ¼ teaspoon salt
- ⅛ teaspoon pepper
- 1 pound ground veal
- ¼ cup butter *or* margarine
- ½ cup chopped carrot
- ¼ cup all-purpose flour
- ½ teaspoon salt
- ⅛ teaspoon pepper
- 2 cups milk *or* light cream
- ¼ cup sliced pitted ripe olives
- ¼ cup dry sherry
- ¼ recipe Spinach Noodles (see recipes, pages 21 and 17) *or* 6 ounces packaged Spinach noodles
  Grated Parmesan cheese

In a bowl stir together the egg and the ⅓ cup milk. Stir in the bread crumbs, the 2 tablespoons Parmesan cheese, ¼ teaspoon salt, and ⅛ teaspoon pepper. Add ground veal; mix well. Shape the veal mixture into 24 meatballs.

In a large skillet cook the meatballs in butter or margarine about 10 minutes or till brown. Remove meatballs; set aside. In the same skillet cook chopped carrot till tender but not brown. Stir in the flour, the ½ teaspoon salt, and ⅛ teaspoon pepper. Add the milk or light cream all at once. Cook and stir till thickened and bubbly. Cook and stir 1 minute more. Stir in pitted ripe olives and dry sherry. Add the meatballs; heat through.

Meanwhile, cook noodles in boiling salted water till *al dente*. Drain in a colander. Serve meatball mixture atop the noodles. Pass additional grated Parmesan cheese. Makes 4 main-dish servings.

MEAT

You can expect to get 24 one-inch meatballs from one pound of ground meat. To make uniform-size meatballs in a fast and simple way, pat meat mixture into a l-inch-thick rectangle and cut into l-inch cubes, then roll cubes into balls. Create larger or smaller meatballs by varying the thickness of the rectangle and the size of the cubes. Or shape the meat mixture into a log and cut off equal-size slices, then roll slices into balls. The diameter of the log should be the same as the diameter you want for the meatballs.

28

SAVORY LASAGNA

- 1 pound ground pork
- ½ cup chopped onion
- ½ cup shredded carrot
- 1 28-ounce can tomatoes, cut up
- ¼ cup dry white wine
- 1 tablespoon dried parsley flakes
- 1 teaspoon instant chicken bouillon granules
- 1 teaspoon dried marjoram, crushed
- 2 tablespoons water
- 1 tablespoon cornstarch
- 3 tablespoons butter *or* margarine
- 3 tablespoons all-purpose flour
- ¼ teaspoon salt
- 1½ cups milk *or* light cream
- 1½ cups shredded Gruyère cheese
- ¾ recipe Basic Lasagna Noodles (see recipes, pages 8 and 16) *or* 10 ounces packaged lasagna noodles

For meat sauce, cook pork, onion, and carrot till the meat is brown and the vegetables are tender. Drain off fat. Stir in the *undrained* tomatoes, wine, parsley flakes, bouillon, marjoram, and ⅛ teaspoon *pepper*. Bring to boiling; reduce heat. Simmer, uncovered, about 45 minutes, stirring occasionally. Combine water and cornstarch; add to mixture. Cook and stir till thickened and bubbly. Cook and stir 2 minutes more. Set aside.

Melt butter. Stir in flour, salt, and dash *pepper*. Add milk all at once. Cook and stir till thickened and bubbly. Cook and stir 1 minute more. Stir in shredded Gruyère cheese till melted. Set aside.

Cook lasagna noodles in boiling salted water till *al dente*. Drain. Rinse with cold water; drain. Arrange a single layer of noodles in bottom of a well-greased 13x9x2-inch baking dish. Spread *half* of the meat sauce atop noodles. Arrange another single layer of noodles atop meat sauce. Top with Gruyère cheese mixture. Arrange the remaining noodles atop Gruyère mixture. Top with remaining meat sauce. Cover; bake in a 350° oven for 30 minutes. Uncover; bake 10 to 15 minutes more. Let stand 10 minutes. Makes 8 main-dish servings.

PIZZA PASTA PIE

6 ounces packaged spaghetti
2 tablespoons butter *or* margarine
2 beaten eggs
⅓ cup grated Parmesan *or* romano cheese
1 cup shredded mozzarella cheese
1 pound hot-style bulk pork sausage
1 cup sliced fresh mushrooms
2 ounces sliced pepperoni, cut in half
½ cup chopped onion
1 clove garlic, minced
1 7½-ounce can tomatoes, cut up
1 6-ounce can tomato paste
1 teaspoon dried oregano, crushed
2 tablespoons grated Parmesan *or* romano cheese

Cook spaghetti in boiling salted water till *al dente*. Immediately drain in a colander. Stir the butter or margarine into the hot spaghetti; stir in the beaten eggs and the ⅓ cup Parmesan or romano cheese. In a greased 10-inch pie plate form the spaghetti mixture into a "crust." Sprinkle shredded mozzarella cheese over the crust.

In a large skillet cook sausage, mushrooms, pepperoni, onion, and garlic till sausage is brown and onion is tender. Drain off fat. Stir in *undrained* tomatoes, tomato paste, and oregano; heat through.

Turn the meat mixture into the crust. Cover the edges with foil. Bake in a 350° oven for 20 minutes. Sprinkle with the 2 tablespoons Parmesan cheese. Bake the pie about 5 minutes more or till cheese is melted. Makes 6 main-dish servings.

MEAT

You can find chinese cabbage and bok choy in the produce sections of your supermarket. Chinese cabbage grows in thick, white stalks with light green fringed leaves. Bok choy, with a flavor similar to cabbage, resembles celery and has large, dark green leaves.

BROCCOLI AND STARS

½ cup finely chopped Chinese cabbage *or* bok choy
½ pound ground pork
1 4½-ounce can shrimp, rinsed, drained, and chopped
1 tablespoon sliced green onion
1 tablespoon soy sauce
1 tablespoon dry sherry
½ teaspoon grated gingerroot
½ recipe Basic Filled Stars (see recipes, pages 8 and 19)
3 tablespoons soy sauce
1 tablespoon cornstarch
½ cup water
2 tablespoons dry sherry
1 teaspoon grated gingerroot
⅛ to ¼ teaspoon crushed red pepper
3 cups broccoli buds
1 tablespoon cooking oil

For filling, fold a double layer of cheese-cloth or paper toweling around the cabbage or bok choy; press tightly to extract as much moisture as possible.

Combine the cabbage or bok choy, ground pork, shrimp, sliced green onion, the 1 tablespoon soy sauce, the 1 tablespoon dry sherry, and the ½ teaspoon grated gingerroot; mix well. Cover and refrigerate till needed.

Fill each star with some of the pork filling according to directions on page 19. Cook stars in boiling salted water about 8 minutes or till filling is done. Immediately drain in a colander; keep warm.

Meanwhile, stir together the 3 tablespoons soy sauce and cornstarch. Stir in water, the 2 tablespoons dry sherry, the 1 teaspoon grated gingerroot, and the crushed red pepper. Set aside. Cook broccoli, covered, in boiling salted water for 2 minutes; drain.

Preheat a large skillet or wok over high heat; add cooking oil. Stir-fry broccoli in hot oil about 2 minutes or till crisp-tender. Stir cornstarch mixture; add to skillet. Cook and stir till thickened and bubbly. Cook and stir 2 minutes more. Add cooked pasta stars; toss gently to coat. Makes 5 main-dish servings.

SAUSAGE AND CHEESE MANICOTTI

¾ pound bulk pork sausage
1 beaten egg
1 cup cream-style cottage cheese
1 cup shredded Monterey Jack
    cheese (4 ounces)
¼ cup snipped parsley
½ teaspoon dried basil, crushed
12 Spinach Manicotti (see recipes,
    pages 21 and 18)
¼ cup sliced green onion
2 tablespoons butter *or* margarine
2 tablespoons all-purpose flour
¼ teaspoon salt
¼ teaspoon dried basil, crushed
    Dash pepper
1¾ cups light cream *or* milk
1½ cups shredded Monterey Jack
    cheese (6 ounces)
1½ cups soft bread crumbs
¼ cup grated Parmesan cheese
¼ cup snipped parsley
2 tablespoons butter *or* margarine,
    melted

For filling, cook bulk pork sausage till brown. Drain off fat. In a bowl, stir together egg, cottage cheese, the 1 cup Monterey Jack cheese, ¼ cup snipped parsley, and the ½ teaspoon basil. Stir in the sausage. Fill each uncooked manicotti with some of the sausage filling according to the directions on page 18. Place the filled manicotti in a greased 13x9x2-inch baking dish.

In a saucepan cook green onion in the 2 tablespoons butter or margarine till tender but not brown. Stir in flour, salt, the ¼ teaspoon basil, and pepper. Add light cream or milk all at once. Cook and stir till thickened and bubbly. Cook and stir 1 minute more. Stir in the 1½ cups Monterey Jack cheese till melted. Pour over the manicotti in baking dish. Cover with foil. Bake in a 350° oven for 20 minutes. Meanwhile, combine the bread crumbs, the grated Parmesan cheese, and ¼ cup snipped parsley. Stir in 2 tablespoons melted butter or margarine; sprinkle the crumb mixture atop manicotti. Bake, uncovered, about 15 minutes longer or till manicotti is *al dente*. Makes 6 main-dish servings.

When preparing stir-fried dishes, substitute a skillet for a wok. Choose a heavy-duty skillet with deep sides and keep the food moving constantly to cook the ingredients quickly and uniformly.

If you don't have time to make your own manicotti, substitute packaged manicotti for the homemade in Sausage and Cheese Manicotti at left. Remember, however, that packaged manicotti requires precooking, and will hold slightly more filling than homemade.

PORK WITH HOISIN SAUCE

1 pound boneless pork
⅔ cup water
2 tablespoons soy sauce
1 tablespoon cornstarch
1 tablespoon hoisin sauce
2 teaspoons dry sherry
1 ounce rice sticks
    Cooking oil *or* shortening for
    deep-fat frying
2 tablespoons sesame oil
½ of a small cucumber

Partially freeze the pork. Slice thinly across the grain into bite-size strips. In a small bowl stir together the water, soy sauce, cornstarch, hoisin sauce, and dry sherry; set the soy mixture aside.

Fry the *unsoaked* rice sticks, a few at a time, in deep hot cooking oil or shortening (375°) about 5 seconds or just till the sticks puff and rise to the top. Use a slotted spoon to remove the rice sticks from the hot cooking oil; drain on paper toweling. Keep warm in a 300° oven.

Preheat a large skillet or wok over high heat; add sesame oil. Stir-fry the pork in hot sesame oil for 2 to 3 minutes or till done. Stir the soy sauce mixture; stir into pork. Cook and stir till thickened and bubbly. Cook and stir 2 minutes more.

Halve the cucumber and scrape out the seeds; finely shred the cucumber. On a large platter arrange the pork mixture atop the rice sticks. Top with shredded cucumber. Makes 4 main-dish servings.

Pork with Hoisin Sauce

SPICY HOT MEAT SAUCE

1 pound bulk Italian sausage
1 clove garlic, minced
½ cup chopped onion
½ cup thinly sliced carrot
1 28-ounce can tomatoes, cut up
1 8-ounce can tomato sauce
½ of a small green pepper, sliced
½ cup sliced celery
2 teaspoons chili powder
1 teaspoon instant beef bouillon granules
½ teaspoon sugar
¼ teaspoon crushed red pepper
½ recipe Parsley Fettuccine (see recipes, pages 23 and 17), Herb Fettuccine (see recipes, pages 22 and 17), *or* 8 ounces packaged fettuccine
Shredded mozzarella cheese

In a Dutch oven cook Italian sausage, garlic, chopped onion, and sliced carrot till meat is browned and vegetables are tender. Drain off fat. Stir in *undrained* tomatoes, tomato sauce, green pepper, celery, chili powder, beef bouillon granules, sugar, and crushed red pepper. Bring to boiling. Reduce heat; simmer, uncovered, about 30 minutes or to desired consistency.

Meanwhile, cook fettuccine in boiling salted water till *al dente.* Immediately drain in a colander. Toss with the sausage mixture. Sprinkle with mozzarella cheese. Makes 4 main-dish servings.

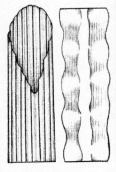

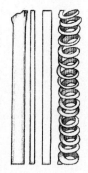

BAKED NOODLE PIE

8 ounces bulk pork sausage
1 medium cooking apple, peeled, cored, and chopped
¼ recipe Basic Noodles (see recipes, pages 8 and 17) *or* 5 ounces packaged medium noodles
2 eggs
½ cup shredded cheddar cheese (2 ounces)
¼ cup fine dry bread crumbs
¼ cup finely chopped onion
1 beaten egg
½ cup cream-style cottage cheese, drained
½ cup shredded cheddar cheese (2 ounces)
Snipped parsley (optional)

In a skillet cook the bulk pork sausage and the chopped apple till sausage is brown; drain off fat. Set aside. Cook the noodles in boiling salted water till *al dente.* Immediately drain in a colander. Rinse with cold water; drain.

Combine the 2 eggs, the ½ cup shredded cheddar cheese, the fine dry bread crumbs, and chopped onion. Pour the egg mixture over the noodles; toss to coat. Turn mixture into a greased 9-inch quiche dish or pie plate.

Combine the 1 beaten egg, cream-style cottage cheese, and ½ cup shredded cheddar cheese; stir in the sausage and apple mixture. Spoon mixture over the noodles in the quiche dish or pie plate. Bake in a 350° oven for 20 to 25 minutes or till mixture is heated through. Let stand 5 minutes before serving. Sprinkle with parsley, if desired. Cut into wedges to serve. Makes 6 main-dish servings.

POT ROAST CARBONNADE

1 3- to 3¼-pound beef chuck pot roast
3 medium onions, sliced and separated into rings
1 12-ounce can (1½ cups) beer
1 tablespoon brown sugar
2 teaspoons instant beef bouillon granules
4 whole black peppercorns *or* ⅛ teaspoon cracked pepper
1 clove garlic, minced
½ teaspoon dried sage, crushed
4 medium carrots, cut into 2-inch pieces
2 tablespoons cornstarch
2 tablespoons water
⅓ recipe Spinach Noodles (see recipes, pages 21 and 17) *or* 12 ounces packaged spinach noodles

Trim excess fat from roast. In a Dutch oven heat trimmings till about 2 tablespoons fat accumulate, adding cooking oil if necessary. Discard the trimmings. Brown the roast slowly on all sides in the hot fat. Cover the meat with the sliced onion rings. Combine beer, brown sugar, bouillon granules, peppercorns or cracked pepper, garlic, and sage. Add to the roast and onions.

Cover and simmer for 1½ hours. Add the carrots and simmer, covered, about 30 minutes more or till the meat and carrots are tender. Remove meat and carrots. Skim fat from juices; measure 2 cups juices. Stir together cornstarch and water. Add to the 2 cups pan juices. Cook and stir till thickened and bubbly. Cook and stir 2 minutes more.

Meanwhile, cook noodles in boiling salted water till *al dente*. Immediately drain in a colander. Arrange meat and carrots atop noodles. Spoon some of the thickened pan juices atop. Pass remainder. Makes 8 main-dish servings.

Rice sticks, which are brittle strands of rice flour, resemble nylon fishing line. When cooked, they puff and expand into crunchy noodles. Rice sticks are available in most Oriental stores and sometimes in the foreign foods section of large supermarkets.

MARINATED BEEF OVER RICE STICKS

1 pound beef top round steak
¼ cup dry sherry
¼ cup soy sauce
1 teaspoon grated gingerroot
1 teaspoon sesame oil
1 clove garlic, minced
2 medium carrots, thinly sliced
2 tablespoons cooking oil
1 6-ounce package frozen pea pods
2 teaspoons cornstarch
1 8-ounce can sliced water chestnuts, drained
Fried Rice Sticks

Partially freeze steak. Slice thinly across the grain into bite-size strips. In a bowl stir together the sherry, soy sauce, grated gingerroot, sesame oil, and garlic. Add the meat, stirring to coat. Cover and let stand at room temperature for 1 hour. Drain, reserving marinade. Add enough *water* to the reserved marinade to equal ⅔ cup mixture. Meanwhile, cook carrots in a small amount of boiling water for 3 minutes. Drain.

Heat cooking oil in a large skillet or wok over high heat. Add *half* of the meat. Stir-fry about 3 minutes or till done. Remove from skillet or wok; set aside. Stir-fry remaining meat about 3 minutes or till done. Remove from skillet or wok. (Add more cooking oil, if necessary.) Stir-fry sliced carrots and pea pods about 2 minutes or till crisp-tender. Stir together the reserved marinade and the cornstarch. Add the marinade mixture and meat to vegetables in skillet or wok. Cook and stir till thickened and bubbly. Stir in water chestnuts. Cook and stir 2 minutes more. Serve meat-vegetable mixture over Fried Rice Sticks. Makes 4 to 6 main-dish servings.

Fried Rice Sticks: Fry 2 ounces *unsoaked rice sticks*, a few at a time, in deep hot *cooking oil* (375°) about 5 seconds or just till sticks puff and rise to top. Remove; drain on paper toweling.

DILLED SWISS STEAK

1 pound beef round steak, cut
 ¾ inch thick
4 teaspoons all-purpose flour
½ teaspoon salt
⅛ teaspoon pepper
2 tablespoons cooking oil
¾ cup water
2 stalks celery, sliced
1 small onion, sliced
1 teaspoon instant beef bouillon
 granules
½ teaspoon Worcestershire sauce
1 tablespoon all-purpose flour
½ teaspoon dried dillweed
½ cup dairy sour cream
¼ recipe Spinach Noodles (see
 recipes, pages 21 and 17) *or*
 8 ounces packaged spinach
 noodles

Cut meat into 4 serving-size pieces. Combine the 4 teaspoons flour, salt, and pepper; pound into the meat. In a 10-inch skillet quickly brown the meat on both sides in hot cooking oil. Add the water, celery, onion, beef bouillon granules, and Worcestershire sauce. Cover and cook over low heat about 1¼ hours or till the meat is tender. Remove the meat; keep warm.

For the sauce, stir the 1 tablespoon flour and the dillweed into the sour cream. Stir the sour cream mixture into the skillet mixture. Cook and stir till thickened and bubbly. Cook and stir 1 minute more.

Meanwhile, cook the noodles in boiling salted water till *al dente*. Immediately drain in a colander. Serve the meat and sauce atop the hot cooked noodles. Makes 4 main-dish servings.

BEEF STROGANOFF

1 pound boneless beef sirloin steak
1 tablespoon all-purpose flour
½ teaspoon salt
2 tablespoons butter *or* margarine
1½ cups sliced fresh mushrooms
½ cup chopped onion
1 clove garlic, minced
2 tablespoons butter *or* margarine
1¼ cups water
1 tablespoon tomato paste
1 teaspoon instant beef bouillon
 granules
¼ teaspoon salt
3 tablespoons all-purpose flour
1 8-ounce carton plain yogurt
½ recipe Basic Farfalle (see recipes,
 pages 8 and 17) *or* 8 ounces
 packaged medium noodles

Partially freeze the steak; slice thinly across the grain into bite-size strips. Combine the 1 tablespoon flour and the ½ teaspoon salt; coat meat with flour mixture. In a skillet heat 2 tablespoons butter or margarine. Add meat; brown quickly, stirring constantly. Add mushrooms, onion, and garlic; cook 2 to 4 minutes or till onion is crisp-tender. Remove the meat-mushroom mixture from skillet. Add 2 tablespoons butter or margarine to drippings in the skillet. Stir in water, tomato paste, bouillon granules, and the ¼ teaspoon salt; mix well. Stir the 3 tablespoons flour into the yogurt; add to mixture in skillet. Cook and stir over medium-high heat till thickened and bubbly. Cook and stir 1 minute more. Return the meat-mushroom mixture to skillet; heat through.

Meanwhile, cook the farfalle or noodles in boiling salted water till *al dente*. Immediately drain in a colander. Serve the meat-mushroom mixture atop the farfalle. Makes 4 main-dish servings.

CHILI OVER FRIED SPAGHETTI

- ¾ pound ground beef
- ¼ cup sliced green onion
- 1 clove garlic, minced
- 1 16-ounce can tomatoes, cut up
- 1 15½-ounce can red kidney beans, drained
- 1 6-ounce can tomato paste
- 1 4-ounce can green chili peppers, rinsed, seeded, and chopped
- ¼ cup chopped celery
- 1 teaspoon sugar
- 1 bay leaf
- ¾ teaspoon dried basil, crushed
- ½ teaspoon salt
  Dash pepper
- 8 ounces packaged spaghetti
- 3 eggs
- ¾ cup shredded cheddar cheese (3 ounces)
- ¼ cup grated Parmesan cheese
- 2 tablespoons sliced green onion
- ¼ teaspoon salt
  Dash pepper
- 2 tablespoons butter or margarine

In a saucepan or Dutch oven cook the ground beef, the ¼ cup sliced onion, and garlic till meat is brown and onion is tender. Drain off fat. Stir in *undrained* tomatoes, kidney beans, tomato paste, green chili peppers, celery, sugar, bay leaf, basil, the ½ teaspoon salt, and dash pepper. Bring to boiling; reduce heat. Cover; simmer about 30 minutes, stirring occasionally.

Meanwhile, cook spaghetti in boiling salted water till *al dente*. Immediately drain in a colander. Rinse with cold water; drain. In a bowl beat together eggs, cheddar cheese, Parmesan cheese, the 2 tablespoons sliced green onion, the ¼ teaspoon salt, and dash pepper. Toss with spaghetti till coated.

Melt the butter or margarine in a heavy-duty 10-inch skillet. Add the spaghetti mixture. Cook without stirring over medium heat about 8 minutes or till bottom is golden. To serve, turn out of skillet, browned side up, and cut into 8 wedges. Spoon the meat mixture over wedges. Makes 8 main-dish servings.

Plan a simple dinner party with the Spaghetti and Meatballs at right as your main course. For an appetizer, offer an antipasto tray with an assortment of cheeses, cold sliced meats, and Italian bread. Accompany the antipasto with glasses of chilled vermouth. Instead of a salad, provide a basket of crisp, fresh vegetables— cauliflower, green onions, radishes, and zucchini—to complement your entrée. For dessert, serve a tray of fruit, such as tangerines and apricots, or pass Italian cookies to accompany espresso coffee.

35

SPAGHETTI AND MEATBALLS

- ¾ cup chopped onion
- ¾ cup finely chopped carrot
- 2 tablespoons butter or margarine
- 2 pounds fresh tomatoes, peeled and cut up (6 medium), or one 16-ounce can tomatoes, cut up
- 1 15-ounce can tomato sauce
- 1½ teaspoons dried marjoram, crushed
- 1 teaspoon instant chicken bouillon granules
- 2 bay leaves
- 1 large clove garlic, minced
- 1 beaten egg
- ¼ cup milk
- ¾ cup soft bread crumbs
- ⅓ cup grated Parmesan cheese
- 3 tablespoons snipped parsley
- ½ teaspoon dried oregano, crushed
- ¼ teaspoon salt
  Dash pepper
- ½ pound bulk pork sausage
- ½ pound ground beef
- ⅓ cup dry red wine
- 8 ounces packaged spaghetti
  Grated Parmesan cheese (optional)

In a Dutch oven cook onion and carrot, covered, in butter about 10 minutes or till tender. Stir in tomatoes, tomato sauce, dried marjoram, bouillon granules, bay leaves, and garlic. Bring to boiling; reduce heat. Simmer, uncovered, to desired consistency (allow 35 to 45 minutes for fresh tomatoes; 15 to 20 minutes for canned tomatoes).

Meanwhile, in a mixing bowl stir together egg and milk. Stir in soft bread crumbs, the ⅓ cup Parmesan cheese, parsley, oregano, salt, and pepper. Add sausage and ground beef; mix well. Shape meat mixture into 24 meatballs. Brown in a skillet; drain off fat. Stir meatballs and wine into the tomato mixture. Bring to boiling. Reduce heat; simmer, uncovered, for 10 to 15 minutes or till meatballs are heated through. Remove bay leaves.

Meanwhile, cook spaghetti in boiling salted water till *al dente*. Drain. Serve tomato-meatball mixture atop spaghetti. Pass additional Parmesan cheese, if desired. Makes 4 or 5 main-dish servings.

MEXICALI MEATBALLS AND SAUCE

1 beaten egg
¼ cup milk
1 cup soft bread crumbs
1 4-ounce can green chili peppers, rinsed, seeded, and chopped
2 tablespoons chopped onion
½ teaspoon salt
1 pound ground beef
¼ cup water
2 tablespoons cornstarch
2 16-ounce cans stewed tomatoes, cut up
1 clove garlic, minced
1 teaspoon instant beef bouillon granules
½ teaspoon dried oregano, crushed
½ teaspoon ground cumin
  Few dashes bottled hot pepper sauce
½ recipe Corn Noodles (see recipes, pages 22 and 17) *or* 8 ounces packaged medium noodles

In a bowl stir together the egg and milk. Stir in the bread crumbs, chili peppers, onion, and salt. Add ground beef; mix well. Shape mixture into 24 meatballs. Place in a shallow baking pan. Bake in a 375° oven for 20 to 25 minutes or till done. Drain off fat.

In a large saucepan combine the water and cornstarch. Stir in *undrained* tomatoes, garlic, beef bouillon granules, dried oregano, cumin, and hot pepper sauce. Cook and stir till thickened and bubbly. Cook and stir 2 minutes more. Stir in the meatballs; heat through.

Meanwhile, cook noodles in boiling salted water till *al dente*. Immediately drain in a colander. Serve tomato mixture and meatballs atop noodles. Makes 4 or 5 main-dish servings.

SAUERBRATEN MEATBALLS OVER SPAETZLE

⅓ cup crushed gingersnaps (8 cookies)
1 8-ounce can tomato sauce
½ cup shredded, peeled apple
½ teaspoon salt
1 pound ground beef
1 cup apple juice
2 tablespoons vinegar
1 teaspoon prepared mustard
  Dash pepper
¼ cup crushed gingersnaps (6 cookies)
1 recipe Spaetzle (see recipe, page 12) *or* one 10-ounce package spaetzle, cooked

In a bowl combine ⅓ cup crushed gingersnaps, *2 tablespoons* of the tomato sauce, the apple, and salt. Add the ground beef; mix well. Shape the meat mixture into 24 meatballs.

In a skillet cook the meatballs till brown. Drain off fat. Combine the remaining tomato sauce, apple juice, vinegar, prepared mustard, and pepper. Pour over meatballs. Bring to boiling; reduce heat. Simmer, covered, about 10 minutes, spooning the tomato mixture over the meatballs occasionally. Remove the meatballs.

Stir the ¼ cup crushed gingersnaps into the tomato mixture. Cook and stir till thickened and bubbly. Return meatballs to the mixture; heat through. Serve over hot cooked spaetzle. Makes 4 or 5 main-dish servings.

HAM AND MUSHROOM GNOCCHI

2 cups milk
¼ cup butter *or* margarine
1 cup milk
¾ cup semolina *or* quick-cooking farina
½ teaspoon salt
½ teaspoon Italian seasoning
2 beaten eggs
½ cup grated Parmesan cheese
2 tablespoons butter *or* margarine, melted
½ cup grated Parmesan cheese
½ pound fully cooked ham, cut into strips
3 cups sliced fresh mushrooms (8 ounces)
½ cup chopped onion
2 tablespoons butter *or* margarine
¼ cup marsala *or* dry sherry
8 cherry tomatoes, quartered

In a saucepan heat the 2 cups milk and the ¼ cup butter or margarine till boiling. Combine the 1 cup milk, the semolina or farina, salt, and Italian seasoning. Pour into boiling milk mixture, stirring constantly. Cook and stir about 5 minutes or till very thick. Remove from heat. Stir about *1 cup* of the hot mixture into eggs; return to mixture in saucepan. Stir in ½ cup Parmesan cheese. Pour mixture into a greased 13x9x2-inch baking dish. Cover; chill at least 1 hour or till firm. For the gnocchi, cut the chilled mixture in half lengthwise, then cut each half into fourths crosswise to make 8 rectangles. Cut each rectangle into 2 triangles (16 total). Place triangles on a greased baking sheet. Brush with 2 tablespoons melted butter. Sprinkle with ½ cup Parmesan cheese. Bake gnocchi in a 425° oven for 25 to 30 minutes or till golden brown.

Meanwhile, cook ham, fresh mushrooms, and onion in 2 tablespoons butter till vegetables are tender. Stir in marsala or sherry; boil rapidly till liquid is reduced by half. Stir in tomatoes. Arrange gnocchi around edge of a platter. Spoon ham mixture into center. Makes 4 to 6 main-dish servings.

To simplify last-minute meal preparation, you can prepare the gnocchi dough up to 24 hours in advance and keep it covered in the refrigerator till cooking time.

PINEAPPLE HAM LOAF WITH PASTA

3 beaten eggs
½ cup unsweetened pineapple juice
1 tablespoon prepared horseradish
½ cup finely crushed saltine crackers (14 crackers)
1 pound ground fully cooked ham
1 pound ground pork
2 tablespoons butter *or* margarine
3 tablespoons brown sugar
2 teaspoons prepared mustard
¼ recipe Pineapple Noodles (see recipes, pages 25 and 17) *or* 6 ounces packaged medium noodles
2 pineapple slices, halved
2 maraschino cherries, halved (optional)

In a bowl combine eggs, pineapple juice, and horseradish; stir in crushed crackers. Add ground ham and ground pork; mix well. In a shallow baking pan shape the meat mixture into an 8x4-inch loaf. Bake loaf in a 350° oven for 65 to 70 minutes or till done.

In a saucepan melt butter or margarine. Stir in brown sugar and mustard. Brush mixture over top of loaf. Meanwhile, cook noodles in boiling salted water till *al dente*. Drain. Transfer ham loaf to a serving platter. Arrange the cooked noodles around the loaf. Arrange the pineapple halves and the maraschino cherry halves, if desired, on top of loaf. Makes 8 main-dish servings.

CUCUMBER-SAUCED MANICOTTI

1 pound ground lamb
¼ cup chopped onion
1 clove garlic, minced
1 beaten egg
½ teaspoon salt
½ teaspoon dried basil, crushed
¼ teaspoon dried rosemary, crushed
8 Parsley Manicotti (see recipes, pages 23 and 18)
3 tablespoons butter *or* margarine
3 tablespoons all-purpose flour
¼ teaspoon salt
  Dash pepper
1⅔ cups milk
½ medium cucumber, seeded and chopped

In a skillet cook ground lamb, onion, and garlic till meat is brown and onion is tender; drain off fat. In a bowl stir together egg, the ½ teaspoon salt, basil, and rosemary. Stir in ground lamb mixture; mix well. Cook manicotti in boiling salted water till *al dente*. Immediately drain in a colander. Rinse with cold water; drain.

For sauce, in a medium saucepan melt butter. Stir in flour, the ¼ teaspoon salt, and pepper. Add milk all at once. Cook and stir over medium heat till thickened and bubbly. Cook and stir 1 minute more. Stir in chopped cucumber. Stir ⅓ of the cucumber sauce into the lamb mixture. Fill each manicotti with some of the lamb mixture according to the directions on page 18. Place filled manicotti in a greased 12x7½x2-inch baking dish. Spoon remaining lamb mixture around the manicotti in the baking dish. Spoon remaining cucumber sauce over manicotti. Bake, covered, in a 350° oven about 25 minutes or till heated through. Makes 4 main-dish servings.

For variety, in the Kumquat- and Couscous-Stuffed Chops at right, substitute four 1-inch-thick pork chops for the lamb chops. Broil pork chops 20 to 25 minutes total.

For added convenience, assemble Cucumber-Sauced Manicotti at left ahead of time and refrigerate for 3 to 24 hours. Before serving, bake, covered, about 40 minutes or till heated through.

KUMQUAT- AND COUSCOUS-STUFFED CHOPS

1 8-ounce jar kumquats
¾ teaspoon instant chicken bouillon granules
¼ cup chopped celery
2 tablespoons sliced green onion
  Dash ground red pepper
¾ cup quick-cooking couscous
8 leg sirloin lamb chops, cut 1 inch thick
3 tablespoons orange marmalade
2 tablespoons steak sauce
1 tablespoon water
1 tablespoon butter *or* margarine
1 tablespoon water
1 kiwi, peeled and sliced

Drain the kumquats, reserving 2 tablespoons syrup. Add enough *water* to syrup to make ⅔ cup liquid. Reserve 3 kumquats for garnish; chop remaining. In a saucepan combine reserved kumquat liquid and bouillon; bring to boiling. Stir in chopped kumquats, celery, onion, and red pepper. Return mixture to boiling. Reduce heat; cover and simmer for 5 minutes. Remove from heat. Stir in couscous. Cover; set aside.

Cut a pocket in each lamb chop by cutting from fat side almost to bone edge. Season cavity with *salt* and *pepper*. Spoon some of the couscous mixture into each pocket. Securely fasten pocket opening with wooden picks. (There will be some couscous left over.) For the glaze, stir together marmalade, steak sauce, and 1 tablespoon water. Place chops on a rack in an unheated broiler pan. Brush chops with glaze. Broil 3 inches from heat for 5 to 8 minutes. Turn and brush with glaze again. Broil 5 to 8 minutes more or to desired doneness. Remove the wooden picks.

Meanwhile, bring butter and 1 tablespoon water to boiling; stir in remaining couscous mixture. Cover; let stand several minutes. Serve with stuffed chops. Garnish chops with whole kumquats, sliced kiwi, and celery leaves, if desired. Makes 4 main-dish servings.

CHICKEN MANICOTTI

8 Herb Manicotti (see recipes, pages 22 and 18)
½ cup chopped celery
¼ cup sliced green onion
2 tablespoons butter *or* margarine
1 cup chopped, cooked chicken
½ cup ricotta cheese
¼ cup chopped walnuts
¼ teaspoon salt
2 tablespoons butter *or* margarine
2 tablespoons all-purpose flour
1 cup milk
1 4-ounce can sliced mushrooms, drained
¼ cup shredded American cheese (1 ounce)
¼ cup dry white wine
Snipped parsley

Cook manicotti in boiling salted water till *al dente*. Immediately drain in a colander. Rinse with cold water; drain.

For filling, in a saucepan cook celery and green onion in 2 tablespoons butter or margarine till tender but not brown. Stir the chopped chicken, ricotta cheese, chopped walnuts, and salt into the celery mixture. Fill each manicotti with some of the chicken mixture according to the directions on page 18. Place the filled manicotti, seam side down, in a 12x7½x2-inch baking dish. Cover and bake in a 350° oven about 20 minutes or till heated through.

Meanwhile, in a saucepan melt 2 tablespoons butter or margarine; stir in flour. Add the milk all at once. Cook and stir till the mixture is thickened and bubbly. Cook and stir for 1 minute more. Stir in sliced mushrooms and shredded American cheese till the cheese is melted. Stir in the wine. Pour over the manicotti. Garnish with snipped parsley. Makes 4 main-dish servings.

Purchase large, tube-shaped manicotti in almost any grocery store or make your own manicotti by following the directions on page 34. Purchased manicotti are cylinders with hollow centers for stuffing. Homemade manicotti are flat rectangles that you fill and roll up yourself. Usually purchased manicotti will hold more filling than this homemade pasta, and consequently, you should plan on using fewer of the purchased manicotti for the same amount of filling.

CHICKEN-FILLED RAVIOLI

1 cup finely chopped, cooked chicken
½ cup cream-style cottage cheese
½ cup shredded carrot
2 teaspoons snipped parsley
Dash ground allspice
24 to 30 Basic Ravioli (see recipes, pages 8 and 14)
2 tablespoons butter *or* margarine, melted
2 tablespoons grated Parmesan cheese *or* romano cheese

For filling, stir together chicken, cottage cheese, carrot, parsley, and allspice. Fill ravioli with the chicken mixture according to the directions on page 14. Cook in boiling salted water till *al dente*. Drain. Transfer to a warm serving dish. Gently toss with butter and Parmesan cheese. Makes 4 main-dish servings.

CREAMED CHICKEN OVER PASTA

½ cup chopped green pepper
2 tablespoons butter *or* margarine
¼ cup all-purpose flour
2 teaspoons instant chicken bouillon granules
2 cups milk
2 cups chopped, cooked chicken
2 tablespoons snipped parsley
¼ cup dry sherry
½ recipe Parsley Fettuccine (see recipes, pages 23 and 17)
2 tablespoons sliced almonds, toasted

In a saucepan cook green pepper in butter or margarine till tender. Stir in flour and bouillon granules. Add milk all at once. Cook and stir till thickened and bubbly. Cook and stir for 1 minute more. Stir in chopped chicken and parsley; heat through. Stir in sherry.

Meanwhile, cook fettuccine in boiling salted water till *al dente*. Immediately drain in a colander. Serve chicken mixture atop hot fettuccine; sprinkle with almonds. Makes 4 main-dish servings.

CACCIATORE STARS

1 cup chopped onion
½ cup chopped celery
1 clove garlic, minced
2 tablespoons olive oil *or* cooking oil
1 16-ounce can tomatoes, cut up
1 4-ounce can sliced mushrooms, drained
¼ cup dry white wine
¼ teaspoon salt
¼ teaspoon dried oregano, crushed
¼ teaspoon dried rosemary, crushed
1 slightly beaten egg
1½ cups chopped, cooked chicken
½ cup ricotta cheese
2 tablespoons grated Romano cheese
½ teaspoon dried basil, crushed
¼ teaspoon onion powder
¼ teaspoon pepper
½ recipe Parsley Stars (see recipes, pages 23 and 19)

In a large saucepan cook chopped onion, chopped celery, and minced garlic in olive oil or cooking oil till tender but not brown. Stir in the *undrained* tomatoes, drained mushrooms, wine, salt, oregano, and rosemary. Bring mixture to boiling. Reduce heat. Cover and simmer for 1 to 1½ hours or to desired consistency, stirring occasionally.

Meanwhile, for filling, stir together the beaten egg, chopped chicken, ricotta cheese, Romano cheese, basil, onion powder, and pepper. Fill each star with some of the chicken mixture according to the directions on page 19. Cook stars in boiling salted water till *al dente*. Immediately drain in a colander. Turn into a serving bowl. Pour tomato mixture over hot filled stars. Serve immediately. Makes 4 to 6 main-dish servings.

Cacciatore is a familiar term in dishes such as veal cacciatore or chicken cacciatore. It comes from an Italian word that indicates cooking with tomatoes and herbs and sometimes wine. In the recipe at left, Cacciatore Stars, you'll find that the chicken- and cheese-filled pasta is topped with a savory sauce containing tomatoes, oregano, rosemary, and white wine.

CHICKEN WITH ITALIAN SAUCE

1 large onion, sliced and separated into rings
2 cloves garlic, minced
2 tablespoons olive oil *or* cooking oil
1 2½- to 3-pound broiler-fryer chicken, cut up
1 8-ounce can tomato sauce
1 7½-ounce can tomatoes, cut up
1 4-ounce can whole mushrooms, drained
1 stalk celery, cut into ½-inch slices
¼ teaspoon dried rosemary, crushed
¼ teaspoon dried thyme, crushed
Dash ground sage
½ recipe Herb Linguine (see recipes, pages 22 and 16) *or* 8 ounces packaged spaghetti

In a large skillet cook onion rings and minced garlic in olive oil or cooking oil till tender but not brown. Remove onion; set aside. Add more oil to skillet, if necessary. In the same skillet brown chicken pieces on all sides over medium heat about 15 minutes. Drain off fat. Return cooked onion to skillet.

Stir together tomato sauce, *undrained* tomatoes, drained mushrooms, celery, rosemary, thyme, and sage. Pour tomato mixture over chicken in skillet. Bring to boiling; reduce heat. Cover and simmer for 30 minutes. Uncover and continue to cook over low heat about 15 minutes more or till the chicken is tender, turning chicken pieces occasionally.

Meanwhile, cook linguine or spaghetti in boiling salted water till *al dente*. Immediately drain in a colander. Transfer pasta to a large serving platter; arrange chicken pieces atop the hot linguine or spaghetti. Skim fat off the tomato mixture; spoon tomato mixture atop the chicken. Makes 6 main-dish servings.

ALGERIAN CHICKEN COUSCOUS

SAFFRON PASTA AND CHICKEN

1 medium onion, sliced and
   separated into rings
2 cloves garlic, minced
2 tablespoons olive oil *or* cooking oil
1 2½- to 3-pound broiler-fryer
   chicken, cut up
1 16-ounce can tomatoes, cut up
2 medium carrots, cut into 1-inch
   pieces
2 stalks celery, cut into 1-inch pieces
1 medium turnip, peeled and cubed
½ teaspoon salt
1 medium zucchini, cut into ½-inch
   pieces
½ cup raisins
1½ cups quick-cooking couscous
3 tablespoons snipped parsley
2 tablespoons water
4 teaspoons cornstarch

In a 12-inch skillet or Dutch oven cook onion and garlic in olive oil or cooking oil till tender but not brown. Remove onion; set aside. Add more oil to the skillet, if necessary. In the same skillet brown chicken pieces on all sides over medium heat for 15 minutes. Drain off fat.

Return onion rings to skillet. Add *undrained* tomatoes, carrots, celery, turnip, and salt. Bring to boiling. Reduce heat; cover and simmer for 30 minutes. Stir zucchini pieces and raisins into chicken mixture. Cover and simmer about 15 minutes more or till the chicken is tender and the vegetables are done.

Meanwhile, prepare couscous according to package directions. Stir in parsley. Spoon the cooked couscous onto a large serving platter. Arrange chicken pieces atop the couscous. Keep warm.

Skim fat from the tomato mixture. Stir together the water and cornstarch; add to the tomato mixture in the skillet. Cook and stir till the mixture is thickened and bubbly. Cook and stir for 2 minutes more. Spoon the thickened tomato mixture atop the chicken and couscous. Makes 6 main-dish servings.

Couscous dishes are native to the North African countries of Morocco, Algeria, and Tunisia. Couscous is a fine semolina or coarsely ground wheat. Until recently, it had to be ground at home; however, due to its increasing popularity, you can now purchase couscous already ground in many grocery stores and health food stores.

1 2½- to 3-pound broiler-fryer
   chicken, cut up
2 tablespoons cooking oil
1½ cups sliced fresh mushrooms
½ cup chopped onion
½ cup chopped celery
1 clove garlic, minced
¼ teaspoon ground cinnamon
1 cup water
½ cup dry white wine
½ recipe Basic Noodles (see recipes,
   pages 8 and 17) *or* 8 ounces
   packaged noodles
1 cup dairy sour cream
2 tablespoons all-purpose flour
¼ teaspoon salt
⅛ teaspoon thread saffron, crushed

In a 12-inch skillet brown chicken pieces in cooking oil on all sides over medium heat for 15 minutes. Season chicken with salt and pepper. Remove chicken pieces from skillet; set aside. Add mushrooms, onion, celery, garlic, and cinnamon to skillet; cook, covered, till vegetables are tender but not brown. Return chicken to skillet. Pour water and wine over chicken. Bring to boiling. Reduce heat; cover and simmer for 35 to 45 minutes or till chicken is tender.

Meanwhile, cook noodles in boiling salted water till *al dente*. Immediately drain in a colander. Spoon onto a serving platter. Remove chicken from skillet; arrange atop noodles. Keep warm.

Skim fat from wine mixture in skillet. Stir together sour cream, flour, salt, and saffron; stir into the wine mixture. Cook and stir over medium heat till thickened and bubbly. Cook and stir for 1 minute more. Spoon atop chicken and noodles. Makes 6 main-dish servings.

TOMATO-CURRY CHICKEN

- 3 whole medium chicken breasts (2¼ pounds)
- 1 cup chopped onion
- 1 tablespoon cooking oil
- 2 to 3 teaspoons curry powder
- ½ teaspoon ground coriander
- ⅛ teaspoon paprika
- 1 8-ounce can tomato sauce
- ¼ cup water
- 2 tablespoons cold water
- 1 tablespoon all-purpose flour
- 6 ounces packaged fusilli *or* packaged spaghetti
- ¼ cup chopped cashews

Skin, halve lengthwise and bone chicken breasts. Use a sharp knife to slice the chicken breasts into ½-inch-wide strips. In a large skillet cook chopped onion in cooking oil till tender but not brown. Stir in curry powder, coriander, and paprika. Stir in tomato sauce and the ¼ cup water. Add the chicken strips, stirring to coat. Bring the chicken mixture to boiling; reduce heat. Cover and simmer for 15 to 20 minutes or till the chicken is tender. Stir together the 2 tablespoons water and flour. Stir into the chicken mixture in the skillet. Cook and stir till the mixture is thickened and bubbly. Cook and stir for 1 minute more.

Meanwhile, cook fusilli or spaghetti in boiling salted water till *al dente*. Immediately drain in a colander. Serve chicken mixture atop hot cooked fusilli or spaghetti. Sprinkle with cashews. Makes 6 main-dish servings.

Curry powder is not a single spice but a ground blend of spices used as a seasoning to impart the characteristic flavor of Indian Cooking. Depending on the manufacturer, each blend of curry powder will differ slightly.

CHICKEN WITH PEANUTS

- 2 whole medium chicken breasts (1½ pounds)
- ¼ cup hoisin sauce
- 1 tablespoon cornstarch
- ½ cup dry sherry
- 2 tablespoons rice wine vinegar *or* white vinegar
- 2 teaspoons sugar
- 6 ounces packaged capellini *or* packaged vermicelli
- 2 tablespoons peanut oil *or* cooking oil
- ½ cup raw peanuts
- ¾ cup chopped green pepper
- 1 clove garlic, minced

Skin, halve lengthwise and bone chicken breasts; cut into 1-inch pieces. Set aside. In a small bowl stir together hoisin sauce and cornstarch; stir in dry sherry, vinegar, and sugar. Set aside.

Cook capellini or vermicelli in boiling salted water till *al dente*. Immediately drain in a colander. Rinse with cold water; drain. Set aside.

Preheat a large skillet or wok over high heat; add peanut oil or cooking oil. Add peanuts and stir-fry for 1 minute. Add green pepper and stir-fry about 2 minutes or till peanuts are lightly browned. Remove peanuts and green pepper; add more oil, if necessary. Add *half* of the chicken to the hot skillet or wok; stir-fry for 2 minutes. Remove from the skillet or wok. Stir-fry remaining chicken and the garlic for 2 minutes. Return all chicken to skillet or wok. Stir hoisin sauce mixture; stir into the chicken mixture in the skillet or wok. Cook and stir till the mixture is thickened and bubbly. Cook and stir for 2 minutes more.

Stir the peanuts, the chopped green pepper, and the cooked capellini or vermicelli into the chicken mixture in the skillet or wok. Cook and stir about 2 minutes more or till the mixture is heated through. Serve immediately. Makes 4 or 5 main-dish servings.

CHICKEN LIVERS WITH SPAGHETTI

1 pound chicken livers, cut up
2 tablespoons olive oil *or* cooking oil
2 tablespoons butter *or* margarine
1½ cups sliced fresh mushrooms
½ cup chopped onion
1 clove garlic, minced
1 16-ounce can tomatoes, cut up
1 8-ounce can tomato sauce
⅓ cup dry white wine
1 teaspoon dried thyme, crushed
½ teaspoon salt
¼ teaspoon ground nutmeg
⅛ teaspoon pepper
10 to 12 ounces packaged spaghetti
¼ cup pine nuts *or* cashews, coarsely chopped

In a 10-inch skillet cook chicken livers in olive oil or cooking oil and butter or margarine over medium high heat about 5 minutes or till livers are just barely pink in the center. Use a slotted spoon to remove from skillet, reserving drippings in skillet; set livers aside. Add mushrooms, onion, and garlic to reserved drippings in skillet; cook till tender but not brown. Stir in the *undrained* tomatoes, tomato sauce, wine, thyme, salt, nutmeg, and pepper. Bring mixture to boiling; reduce heat. Simmer, uncovered, for 15 to 20 minutes or till slightly thickened. Stir in chicken livers; heat through.

Meanwhile, cook spaghetti in boiling salted water till *al dente*. Immediately drain in a colander. Serve chicken liver mixture atop the hot cooked spaghetti. Sprinkle with pine nuts or cashews. Makes 5 or 6 main-dish servings.

Cooking oils come from many different sources, such as corn, walnuts, cottonseed, sesame seed, or olives. Each source lends its own distinct aroma and flavor to the cooking oil, and consequently, the foods cooked in the different oils will differ slightly in flavor. Even within a category of oils, such as olive oil, each brand will differ—some will be heavy and strong-flavored, while others will be finer and more delicate.

TURKEY-NOODLE SALAD

¼ recipe Carrot Noodles (see recipes, pages 20 and 17) *or* 4 ounces packaged medium noodles
2 cups chopped, cooked turkey
1 cup seedless green grapes, halved
2 ounces crumbled blue cheese
¼ cup chopped celery
3 tablespoons sliced green onion
½ cup mayonnaise *or* salad dressing
½ cup cream-style cottage cheese
¼ cup milk
2 tablespoons lemon juice
Lettuce leaves
¼ cup slivered almonds, toasted

Cook noodles in boiling salted water till *al dente*. Immediately drain in a colander. Rinse with cold water; drain.

In a mixing bowl combine the chopped turkey, green grape halves, crumbled blue cheese, celery, green onion, and cooked noodles. Set the turkey-noodle mixture aside.

For dressing, in a blender container combine the mayonnaise or salad dressing, cream-style cottage cheese, milk, and lemon juice. Cover and blend just till the mixture is nearly smooth. Pour the dressing over the turkey-noodle mixture; toss gently to coat. Cover and chill in the refrigerator for at least 2 hours.

Turn the turkey-noodle mixture into a lettuce-lined serving bowl. Sprinkle with toasted slivered almonds. Makes 4 or 5 main-dish servings.

PASTA SALAD NICOISE

⅓ cup salad oil
3 tablespoons lemon juice
2 tablespoons vinegar
½ teaspoon salt
½ teaspoon dry mustard
½ teaspoon paprika
½ teaspoon dried basil, crushed
½ recipe Herb Linguine (see recipes, pages 22 and 16) *or* 8 ounces packaged linguine
1 9-ounce package frozen French-style green beans, cooked, drained, and chilled
1 cup cherry tomatoes, halved
¼ cup sliced pitted ripe olives
1 12½-ounce can tuna, chilled and drained
3 hard-cooked eggs, sliced

For salad dressing, in a screw-top jar combine salad oil, lemon juice, vinegar, salt, mustard, paprika, and dried basil. Cover and shake well to mix; set aside.

Cook linguine in boiling salted water till *al dente*. Immediately drain in a colander. Rinse with cold water; drain. Pour salad dressing over cooked linguine; toss gently to coat. Cover and chill in the refrigerator for several hours.

In a salad bowl combine the chilled linguine mixture, green beans, cherry tomato halves, and sliced ripe olives; toss gently to mix. Break tuna into bite-size chunks; mound atop the linguine mixture. Arrange the sliced eggs around the tuna. Toss gently before serving. Makes 6 main-dish servings.

Colorful Pasta Salad Niçoise is a variation of the traditional Salad Niçoise first made in the French port city of Nice.

The original Salad Niçoise was served as either an hors d'oeuvre or a main dish in hot weather. It included lettuce, tomatoes, olives, hard-cooked eggs, cooked green beans, and tuna.

BAKED CAVATELLI WITH SALMON

4 ounces packaged cavatelli
⅓ cup chopped celery
¼ cup chopped onion
2 tablespoons butter *or* margarine
2 tablespoons all-purpose flour
⅛ teaspoon paprika
Dash pepper
1½ cups milk
1 cup shredded Monterey Jack cheese (4 ounces)
1 tablespoon snipped chives
2 teaspoons lemon juice
1 7¾-ounce can salmon, drained, flaked, and skin and bones removed, *or* one 6½-ounce can tuna, drained and flaked
¾ cup soft bread crumbs
2 tablespoons grated Parmesan cheese
2 tablespoons butter *or* margarine, melted

Cook cavatelli in boiling salted water till *al dente*. Immediately drain in a colander. Rinse with cold water; drain.

For sauce, in a saucepan cook celery and onion in 2 tablespoons butter or margarine till tender but not brown. Stir in flour, paprika, and pepper. Add milk all at once. Cook and stir till mixture is thickened and bubbly. Cook and stir for 1 minute more. Stir in the Monterey Jack cheese, chives, and lemon juice, stirring till cheese is melted.

Combine the cooked cavatelli, sauce, and salmon or tuna; toss gently to mix. Turn into a greased 8x1½-inch round baking dish. Stir together the bread crumbs, Parmesan cheese, and the 2 tablespoons melted butter or margarine; sprinkle atop salmon mixture. Bake in a 350° oven for 20 to 25 minutes or till heated through. Makes 4 main-dish servings.

Pasta Salad Niçoise

CANNELLONI WITH WILD RICE AND SALMON

⅓ cup wild rice
1 15½-ounce can salmon, drained, flaked, and skin and bones removed
½ cup dairy sour cream
24 Basic Cannelloni (see recipes, pages 8 and 18) *or* 8 packaged manicotti
2 tablespoons butter *or* margarine
2 tablespoons all-purpose flour
¼ teaspoon salt
Dash pepper
1½ cups light cream *or* milk
⅓ cup shredded Swiss cheese
¼ cup dry white wine
Dried dillweed *or* snipped fresh dill (optional)

For filling, cook wild rice according to package directions. Stir together cooked rice, salmon, and sour cream. Set aside.

Cook cannelloni or manicotti in boiling salted water till *al dente.* Immediately drain in a colander. Rinse with cold water; drain. Fill each cannelloni with some of the salmon filling according to the directions on page 18. Or, spoon about ⅓ cup of the salmon filling into each manicotti. Arrange the filled cannelloni or manicotti in a greased 12x7½x2-inch baking dish.

For sauce, in a saucepan melt the butter or margarine. Stir in the flour, salt, and pepper. Add the light cream or milk all at once. Cook and stir till the mixture is thickened and bubbly. Cook and stir for 1 minute more. Add the shredded Swiss cheese and wine, stirring till the cheese is melted. Pour over the filled cannelloni or manicotti in the baking dish. Cover the dish with foil. Bake in a 350° oven for 25 to 30 minutes or till heated through. Garnish with dillweed or fresh dill, if desired. Makes 6 to 8 main-dish servings.

Cannelloni and manicotti are two different Italian pastas that are often confused with each other. Though they are both made from the same size rectangle, they are rolled differently. Cannelloni are rolled starting at the short end and manicotti are rolled from one corner.

SALMON SWISS SOUFFLE

⅛ recipe Parsley Noodles (see recipes, pages 23 and 17), broken into ½-inch pieces, *or* 2 ounces packaged medium noodles, broken into ½-inch pieces
2 tablespoons sliced green onion
2 tablespoons butter *or* margarine
2 tablespoons all-purpose flour
¼ teaspoon dried dillweed
Dash pepper
1 cup light cream *or* milk
1 cup shredded Swiss cheese (4 ounces)
2 egg yolks
1 7¾-ounce can salmon, drained, flaked, and skin and bones removed
4 egg whites

Attach a foil collar to a 1-quart soufflé dish. For collar, measure enough foil to go around the dish plus a 2- to 3-inch overlap. Fold foil into thirds lengthwise. Lightly butter one side. With buttered side in, position foil around outside of dish. Fasten with tape; set aside. Cook noodles in boiling salted water till *al dente.* Immediately drain in a colander. Rinse with cold water; drain.

Cook green onion in butter or margarine till tender but not brown. Stir in flour, dillweed, and pepper. Add the light cream or milk all at once. Cook and stir till the mixture is thickened and bubbly. Cook and stir for 1 minute more. Add the Swiss cheese, stirring till the cheese is melted. Remove from heat.

Beat the egg yolks till thick and lemon colored. Slowly add the cheese mixture to the egg yolks, stirring constantly. Fold the cooked noodles and salmon into the cheese-yolk mixture.

Using clean beaters, beat egg whites till stiff peaks form (tips stand straight). Gradually fold the cheese-yolk mixture into the beaten egg whites. Pour into the prepared soufflé dish. Bake in a 350° oven for 45 to 50 minutes or till a knife inserted near the center comes out clean. Makes 4 main-dish servings.

BAKED PASTA AND SALMON

½ recipe Basic Farfalle (see recipes, pages 8 and 17) *or* 8 ounces packaged farfalle
1 medium zucchini, chopped
2 tablespoons butter *or* margarine
2 tablespoons all-purpose flour
¼ teaspoon salt
¼ teaspoon paprika
¼ teaspoon dry mustard
⅛ teaspoon ground red pepper
1½ cups milk
1½ cups shredded process Swiss cheese (6 ounces)
1 15½-ounce can salmon, drained, skin and bones removed, and broken into medium chunks
Paprika

Cook farfalle in boiling salted water till *al dente*. Immediately drain in a colander. Rinse with cold water; drain.

In a saucepan cook the chopped zucchini in butter or margarine for 4 to 5 minutes or just till tender. Stir in the flour, salt, the ¼ teaspoon paprika, dry mustard, and ground red pepper. Add the milk all at once. Cook and stir till the zucchini mixture is thickened and bubbly. Cook and stir for 1 minute more. Add the shredded Swiss cheese, stirring till melted. Combine the cooked farfalle, the zucchini mixture, and the salmon; toss gently to mix.

Turn the salmon mixture into a 10x6x2-inch baking dish. Sprinkle with additional paprika. Bake, covered, in a 350° oven for 35 to 40 minutes or till the salmon mixture is heated through. Makes 6 main-dish servings.

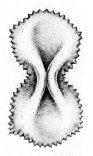

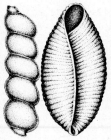

Farfalle is an Italian pasta that looks like little butterflies or bow ties and is sometimes referred to by those names. If you can't find farfalle in your grocery store and don't want to make homemade farfalle, you can substitute 8 ounces of elbow macaroni, corkscrew macaroni, medium shells, or any other medium-size pasta for Baked Pasta and Salmon at left.

MEDITERRANEAN SPAGHETTI

1 pound fresh *or* frozen fish fillets
1 medium green pepper, cut into strips
1 clove garlic, minced
2 tablespoons olive oil *or* cooking oil
1 16-ounce can tomatoes, cut up
1 8-ounce can tomato sauce
¾ cup dry red wine
¼ cup snipped parsley
1 teaspoon sugar
½ teaspoon dried basil, crushed
½ teaspoon dried oregano, crushed
½ cup chopped pitted ripe olives
1 2-ounce can anchovy fillets, drained and cut up
10 ounces packaged spaghetti

Thaw fish fillets, if frozen. In a 3-quart saucepan cook green pepper strips and garlic in olive oil or cooking oil till tender but not brown. Stir in *undrained* tomatoes, tomato sauce, wine, parsley, sugar, basil, and oregano. Bring to boiling; reduce heat. Simmer, uncovered, for 45 to 50 minutes, stirring occasionally.

Remove any skin from fish fillets and cut fillets into 1-inch pieces. Press on paper toweling to remove excess moisture. Stir fish pieces into tomato mixture. Cover and simmer for 5 to 7 minutes or till fish flakes easily when tested with a fork. Gently stir in olives and anchovy fillets; heat through.

Meanwhile, cook the spaghetti in boiling salted water till *al dente.* Immediately drain the spaghetti in a colander. Serve fish mixture atop spaghetti. Makes 5 main-dish servings.

CRAB MANICOTTI WITH GRUYERE SAUCE

8 Basic Manicotti (see recipes, pages 8 and 18) *or* Parsley Manicotti (see recipes, pages 23 and 18)
1 6-ounce can crab meat, drained, flaked, and cartilage removed
¼ cup mayonnaise *or* salad dressing
½ of a 10-ounce package frozen asparagus spears, thawed and drained
2 tablespoons butter *or* margarine
2 tablespoons all-purpose flour
1¼ cups light cream *or* milk
½ teaspoon Dijon-style mustard
½ cup shredded Gruyère cheese (2 ounces)
2 teaspoons lemon juice

Cook manicotti in boiling salted water till *al dente*. Immediately drain in a colander. Rinse with cold water; drain.

For filling, stir together the crab meat and the mayonnaise or salad dressing. Fill each manicotti with some of the crab filling and 1 or 2 asparagus spears according to the directions on page 18. Arrange the filled manicotti in a 12x7½x2-inch baking dish.

For sauce, in a saucepan melt the butter or margarine. Stir in the flour. Add the light cream or milk and the mustard all at once. Cook and stir till the mixture is thickened and bubbly. Cook and stir for 1 minute more. Add the Gruyère cheese and the lemon juice; stir till the cheese is melted.

Pour the sauce over the filled manicotti in baking dish. Cover with foil. Bake in a 350° oven for 20 to 25 minutes or till heated through. Makes 4 main-dish servings.

Gruyère cheese is a form of Swiss cheese that varies from being slightly dry, mealy, acidic, and strong-flavored to being creamy, smooth, and mild-flavored. Usually the creamy Gruyère is a process cheese and will make a smoother and more attractive sauce than the dry natural Gruyère cheese.

CRAB IMPERIAL ON FRIED WONTONS

10 Wontons (see recipe, page 10) *or* 10 packaged wonton skins
Cooking oil for deep-fat frying
¼ cup chopped green pepper
3 tablespoons butter *or* margarine
2 tablespoons all-purpose flour
½ teaspoon dried thyme, crushed
¼ teaspoon salt
⅛ teaspoon paprika
⅛ teaspoon pepper
1½ cups milk *or* light cream
1 6-ounce package frozen crab meat, thawed, *or* one 6-ounce can crab meat, drained, flaked, and cartilage removed
1 tablespoon chopped pimiento

Cut the wonton skins into ¼-inch-wide strips. Fry the wonton strips, a few at a time, in deep hot cooking oil (365°) for ½ to 1 minute or till crisp and golden, stirring occasionally. Drain well on paper toweling. Keep the fried wonton strips warm in a 200° oven.

Cook green pepper in butter or margarine till tender. Stir in flour, thyme, salt, paprika, and pepper. Add milk or light cream all at once. Cook and stir till the mixture is thickened and bubbly. Cook and stir for 1 minute more. Stir in the crab meat and the chopped pimiento. Heat through. Serve over hot fried wonton strips. Makes 3 main-dish servings.

ELEGANT SHRIMP-SAUCED FETTUCCINE

- 1 pound fresh *or* frozen shelled shrimp
- 1 9-ounce package frozen artichoke hearts
- ½ recipe Parsley Fettuccine (see recipes, pages 23 and 17)
- 3 tablespoons butter *or* margarine
- 3 tablespoons all-purpose flour
- ½ teaspoon paprika
- ¼ teaspoon salt
- ¼ teaspoon dried basil, crushed
- ¼ teaspoon dried oregano, crushed
   Dash pepper
- 1½ cups milk
- 1 cup shredded Swiss cheese (4 ounces)
- ¼ cup dry white wine

Drop fresh or frozen shrimp into 3 cups boiling salted water; reduce heat and simmer for 1 to 3 minutes or till shrimp turn pink. Drain.

Cook the artichoke hearts according to package directions; drain. Cook the fettuccine in boiling salted water till *al dente*. Immediately drain in a colander.

Meanwhile, in a medium saucepan melt butter or margarine. Stir in flour, paprika, salt, basil, oregano, and pepper. Add milk all at once. Cook and stir till thickened and bubbly. Cook and stir 1 minute more. Add the shredded cheese; stir till melted. Stir in dry white wine, cooked shrimp, and artichoke hearts; heat through. Serve atop hot cooked fettuccine. Makes 4 main-dish servings.

OCEANFRONT SHELLS

- 1 pint shucked oysters *or* two 8-ounce cans whole oysters
- ½ cup chopped onion
- ¼ cup chopped celery
- 2 tablespoons butter *or* margarine
- 3 tablespoons all-purpose flour
- ⅛ teaspoon pepper
- ¼ cup whipping cream
- 2 tablespoons chopped pimiento
- 2 tablespoons dry white wine
- 1 teaspoon lemon juice
- 18 packaged conchiglioni (jumbo shells)
- 3 tablespoons grated Parmesan cheese

Drain oysters, reserving ½ cup liquid. Coarsely chop oysters. Set aside.

In a saucepan cook onion and celery in butter or margarine till tender but not brown. Stir in flour and pepper. Add the reserved oyster liquid and the whipping cream all at once. Cook and stir till the mixture is thickened and bubbly. Cook and stir for 1 minute more. Stir in chopped oysters, pimiento, wine, and lemon juice; heat through.

Meanwhile, cook conchiglioni in boiling salted water till *al dente*. Immediately drain in a colander. Rinse with cold water; drain.

Fill each conchiglioni with about 2 tablespoons of the oyster mixture. Place the filled shells in a greased 12x7½x2-inch baking dish. Sprinkle the shells with grated Parmesan cheese. Cover with foil. Bake in a 350° oven about 30 minutes or till heated through. Makes 4 main-dish servings.

SPICY SEASIDE STEW

- 1 pound fresh *or* frozen fish fillets
- 8 clams in shells, rinsed, *or* one 10-ounce can whole baby clams
- 1 cup chopped onion
- 1 clove garlic, minced
- 1 tablespoon olive oil *or* cooking oil
- 1 28-ounce can tomatoes, cut up
- 1 15-ounce can tomato juice
- 1 8-ounce bottle clam juice
- ½ cup snipped parsley
- 1 teaspoon finely shredded lemon peel
- ½ teaspoon dried basil, crushed
- ¼ teaspoon crushed red pepper
- ¼ recipe Basic Tortellini, unstuffed (see recipes, pages 8 and 13), *or* 4 ounces packaged conchiglie (medium shells)

Thaw fish fillets, if frozen. Remove any skin from fillets and cut into 1-inch chunks; set aside. If using clams in shells, thoroughly wash clams. Cover with 8 cups cold *water* and 3 tablespoons *salt*. Let stand for 15 minutes; rinse. Repeat soaking and rinsing twice. If using canned clams, drain and reserve liquid (about ½ cup); set aside.

In a 4½-quart kettle or Dutch oven cook onion and garlic in olive oil or cooking oil till onion is tender but not brown. Stir in *undrained* tomatoes, tomato juice, bottled clam juice, parsley, lemon peel, basil, and red pepper. If using clams in shells, add ½ cup *water* or an additional ½ cup *bottled clam juice*. If using canned clams, add the reserved clam liquid. Bring mixture to boiling; reduce heat. Cover and simmer the mixture for 25 minutes.

Stir in the fish pieces, the clams, and the tortellini or conchiglie. Return to boiling; reduce heat. Cover and simmer for 5 to 10 minutes more or till fish flakes easily when tested with a fork and tortellini or conchiglie is *al dente*. Makes 5 main-dish servings.

To make Spicy Seaside Stew with the same pasta ingredient used in the photograph, prepare homemade unstuffed tortellini. For tortellini, just follow the directions on page 13, ignoring all references to the filling. Cut the pasta into squares and fold them according to the directions.

SEAFOOD AND TINY PASTA STEW

- 1 pound fresh *or* frozen fish fillets
- 12 ounces fresh *or* frozen shelled shrimp
- ¾ cup chopped onion
- 2 cloves garlic, minced
- 2 tablespoons olive oil *or* cooking oil
- 2 16-ounce cans tomatoes, cut up
- 4 ounces packaged orzo (⅔ cup) *or* packaged rosamarina (⅔ cup)
- ½ cup dry white wine
- 2 teaspoons dried oregano, crushed
- 1 9-ounce package frozen artichoke hearts, thawed
- 1 green pepper, cut into strips

Thaw the fish fillets, if frozen. Remove any skin from the fillets and cut into 1½-inch pieces; set aside. Thaw the shelled shrimp, if frozen.

In a large saucepan or Dutch oven cook chopped onion and minced garlic in olive oil or cooking oil till onion is tender but not brown. Stir in *undrained* tomatoes, orzo or rosamarina, dry white wine, and dried oregano. Bring the tomato mixture to boiling.

Gently stir the fish fillet pieces and the artichoke hearts into the tomato mixture. Reduce heat. Simmer, uncovered, for 5 minutes. Gently stir in the shrimp and the green pepper. Simmer, uncovered, for 1 to 3 minutes more or till the shrimp turn pink, stirring occasionally. Makes 8 main-dish servings.

MARINER'S CHOWDER

3 ounces packaged cavatelli
1 8-ounce can whole oysters
2 medium potatoes, peeled and cubed
1 medium carrot, sliced
1 medium onion, chopped
1 clove garlic, minced
1 tablespoon butter *or* margarine
½ cup milk
3 tablespoons all-purpose flour
2 cups milk
1 6-ounce package frozen cooked shrimp
¼ teaspoon dried thyme, crushed
¼ teaspoon pepper
⅛ teaspoon ground nutmeg

Cook cavatelli in boiling salted water till *al dente*. Immediately drain in a colander. Rinse with cold water; drain. Set the cavatelli aside.

Drain oysters, reserving liquid. Add enough *water* to the reserved oyster liquid to measure 2 cups total liquid.

In a large saucepan cook potatoes and carrot slices, covered, in the reserved oyster liquid about 15 minutes or till the potatoes are tender and the carrot slices are crisp-tender. Meanwhile, in a skillet cook the onion and garlic in butter or margarine till tender but not brown.

Stir together the ½ cup milk and the flour; stir into the potato mixture. Stir in the cooked cavatelli, oysters, onion mixture, the 2 cups milk, frozen shrimp, thyme, pepper, and nutmeg. Cook and stir till the mixture is slightly thickened and bubbly. Cook and stir for 1 minute more. Makes 4 or 5 main-dish servings.

Chowders are traditionally thick soups or stews that are made with any combination of fish, seafood, or vegetables.

HONOLULU SEAFOOD SALAD

¼ recipe Pineapple Noodles (see recipes, pages 25 and 17) *or* 6 ounces packaged medium noodles
1 medium avocado, halved, seeded, and peeled
Lemon juice
1 15½-ounce can pineapple chunks, drained
1 7-ounce can crab meat, drained, flaked, and cartilage removed
1 4½-ounce can shrimp, rinsed and drained
½ cup mayonnaise *or* salad dressing
¼ cup dairy sour cream
3 tablespoons sliced green onion
2 tablespoons chili sauce
½ teaspoon Worcestershire sauce
¼ teaspoon dry mustard
Dash bottled hot pepper sauce
Lettuce leaves
¼ cup broken pecans

Cook noodles in boiling salted water till *al dente*. Immediately drain in a colander. Rinse with cold water; drain.

Slice avocado crosswise; brush with lemon juice to prevent darkening. In a mixing bowl combine the cooked noodles, avocado slices, pineapple chunks, crab meat, and shrimp.

For dressing, stir together mayonnaise or salad dressing, sour cream, sliced green onion, chili sauce, Worcestershire sauce, dry mustard, and bottled hot pepper sauce. Spoon dressing over the seafood mixture; toss gently to coat. Cover and chill in the refrigerator for at least 2 hours. Serve on individual lettuce-lined plates. Sprinkle each serving with broken pecans. Makes 4 main-dish servings.

CRAB SALAD-FILLED SEASHELLS

12 packaged conchiglioni (jumbo shells)
⅔ cup dairy sour cream
¼ cup chopped green pepper
2 tablespoons snipped chives or sliced green onion
2 7-ounce cans crab meat, drained, flaked, and cartilage removed
1 medium tomato, peeled, seeded, and chopped
½ cup finely chopped celery
Paprika
Lettuce leaves

Cook the packaged conchiglioni in boiling salted water till *al dente*. Immediately drain in a colander. Rinse with cold water; drain.

For filling, in a mixing bowl stir together the dairy sour cream, chopped green pepper, and snipped chives or sliced green onion. Gently fold in the flaked crab meat, chopped tomato, and finely chopped celery.

Spoon about ¼ cup of the crab meat filling into each cooked conchiglioni. Sprinkle the top of each jumbo shell with a little paprika.

Place the filled conchiglioni in a tightly covered container and chill in the refrigerator for at least 2 hours. Place 3 filled conchiglioni on each of 4 individual lettuce-lined salad plates. Makes 4 main-dish servings.

Chives, used in Crab Salad-Filled Seashells at left, are the mildest-flavored member of the onion family. Keep a pot of these hollow grasslike plants growing in your kitchen and enjoy fresh chives throughout the year.

LOBSTER AND LINGUINE WITH CITRUS BUTTER

¼ recipe Orange Linguine (see recipes, pages 24 and 16) *or* 6 ounces packaged linguine
3 tablespoons butter *or* margarine
1 tablespoon snipped parsley
1 tablespoon lemon juice *or* orange juice
⅛ teaspoon ground ginger
1 6½-ounce can lobster, drained, broken into large pieces, and cartilage removed
Lemon slices or orange slices (optional)

Cook linguine in boiling salted water till *al dente*. Immediately drain the cooked linguine in a colander.

Meanwhile, in a small saucepan melt the butter or margarine. Stir the snipped parsley, lemon juice or orange juice, and ground ginger into the melted butter or margarine.

In a mixing bowl combine the drained lobster pieces and the hot cooked linguine. Drizzle the lemon juice-butter mixture atop the lobster and linguine; toss gently to coat the lobster and linguine with the lemon juice-butter mixture.

Tranfer the lobster mixture to a serving platter. Garnish with lemon slices or orange slices, if desired. Makes 3 main-dish servings.

LINGUINE WITH BEER-CHEESE SAUCE

½ recipe Diable Linguine (see recipes, pages 23 and 16) *or* 8 ounces packaged linguine
⅓ cup chopped onion
3 tablespoons butter *or* margarine
3 tablespoons all-purpose flour
1 teaspoon instant beef bouillon granules
¼ teaspoon pepper
1½ cups milk
1½ cups shredded American cheese (6 ounces)
½ cup shredded cheddar cheese (2 ounces)
⅓ cup beer
1 tablespoon snipped parsley (optional)

Cook linguine in boiling salted water till *al dente*. Immediately drain in a colander. Meanwhile, for cheese sauce in a medium saucepan cook chopped onion in butter or margarine till tender but not brown. Stir in flour, beef bouillon granules, and pepper. Add milk all at once. Cook and stir till mixture is thickened and bubbly. Cook and stir 1 minute more. Stir in shredded American cheese, shredded cheddar cheese, and beer, stirring till the American cheese and cheddar cheese are melted. Serve the cheese sauce atop the hot cooked linguine. Sprinkle with snipped parsley, if desired. Makes 4 main-dish servings.

If you've ever wondered what the correct way is to eat long pasta such as fettuccine, spaghetti, or linguine, you're not alone. Famous chefs and etiquette experts have disagreed for years. Some say use a fork to spear a few strands of pasta and then place the tips of the fork against a large spoon. Next, holding the spoon on its side in one hand, use your other hand to twirl the fork against the spoon. Others spear long pasta on the tines of a fork and twirl it around the fork while the fork is resting against the curved indentation of the plate.

FETTUCCINE WITH BROCCOLI-CHEESE SAUCE

¾ recipe Herb Fettuccine (see recipes, pages 22 and 17)
¾ pound broccoli *or* one 10-ounce package frozen cut broccoli, thawed
2 medium carrots, thinly sliced
2 tablespoons butter *or* margarine
3 tablespoons all-purpose flour
3 tablespoons snipped chives
¾ teaspoon instant chicken bouillon granules
⅛ teaspoon white pepper
2 cups milk
1½ cups shredded Monterey Jack cheese (6 ounces)
¾ cup shredded Gruyère cheese (3 ounces)
3 tablespoons dry white wine

Cook fettuccine in boiling salted water till *al dente*. Immediately drain in a colander. Meanwhile, if using fresh broccoli, remove and discard any thick stems and leaves; cut up. Cook fresh broccoli and the carrots in a small amount of boiling salted water about 5 minutes or till crisp-tender. Drain well. If using frozen broccoli, *do not* cook the broccoli; cook *only* the carrots in boiling salted water about 5 minutes or till the carrots are crisp-tender. Drain well.

In a medium saucepan melt the butter or margarine. Stir in the flour, snipped chives, chicken bouillon granules, and white pepper. Add the milk all at once. Cook and stir till the mixture is thickened and bubbly. Cook and stir 1 minute more. Stir in the shredded Monterey Jack cheese and the shredded Gruyère cheese just till melted. Stir in the dry white wine, cooked or thawed broccoli, and cooked carrots; heat through. Serve atop the hot cooked fettuccine. Makes 4 main-dish servings.

SWISS-SAUCED FETTUCCINE

- ¼ recipe Tomato Fettuccine (see recipes, pages 24 and 17) *or* ¼ recipe Carrot Fettuccine (see recipes, pages 20 and 17) *or* 8 ounces packaged fettuccine
- 8 slices bacon, cut into 1-inch pieces
- ½ pound asparagus, cut into 1-inch pieces, *or* one 8-ounce package frozen cut asparagus
- 1 tablespoon all-purpose flour
- ¼ teaspoon salt
  Dash pepper
- 1 cup light cream *or* milk
- 1 cup shredded process Swiss cheese (4 ounces)
- 6 hard-cooked eggs, sliced

Cook fettuccine in boiling salted water till *al dente.* Immediately drain in a colander. Meanwhile, in a saucepan cook bacon till crisp. Drain bacon, reserving 2 tablespoons drippings in the saucepan. Set bacon aside. In the same saucepan cook asparagus in the bacon drippings about 5 minutes or till tender. Remove asparagus, reserving drippings in the saucepan. Set asparagus aside.

For cheese sauce stir the flour, salt, and pepper into the drippings in the saucepan. Add light cream or milk all at once. Cook and stir till the mixture is thickened and bubbly. Cook and stir 1 minute more. Stir in the shredded Swiss cheese till melted.

Toss together the cooked fettuccine, bacon, asparagus, and egg slices. Pour cheese sauce over all; toss gently. Makes 4 main-dish servings.

EGG AND VEGETABLE PRIMAVERA

- 6 ounces packaged linguine
- 2 medium carrots, very thinly bias-sliced
- ½ cup chopped onion
- 1 clove garlic, minced
- 1 teaspoon dried thyme, crushed
- ¼ teaspoon salt
- ⅛ teaspoon pepper
- 3 tablespoons butter *or* margarine
- 1 6-ounce package frozen pea pods, thawed
- ¾ cup cashews
- ¼ cup dry white wine
- ⅓ cup grated Parmesan cheese
- 6 hard-cooked eggs, sliced

Cook linguine in boiling salted water till *al dente.* Immediately drain the linguine in a colander.

Meanwhile, in a 10-inch skillet cook the bias-sliced carrots, chopped onion, minced garlic, dried thyme, salt, and pepper in the butter or margarine about 6 minutes or till the carrots are crisp-tender. Stir in the thawed pea pods, cashews, and dry white wine. Cook over medium heat for 1 to 2 minutes or till the carrot mixture is heated through.

Toss together cooked linguine, carrot mixture, and grated Parmesan cheese. Evenly divide linguine mixture among 4 individual serving plates. Arrange some of the sliced hard-cooked eggs atop each. Makes 4 main-dish servings.

BRIE PASTA SOUFFLE

2 ounces packaged medium noodles, broken into ½-inch pieces
¼ cup shredded carrot
2 tablespoons sliced green onion
2 tablespoons butter *or* margarine
2 tablespoons all-purpose flour
¼ teaspoon salt
⅛ teaspoon ground nutmeg
1 cup light cream *or* milk
1 5¼-ounce can Brie cheese, rind removed and cubed
¼ cup grated Parmesan cheese
2 egg yolks
4 egg whites

Attach a foil collar to a 1-quart soufflé dish. For collar, measure enough foil to go around the dish plus a 2- to 3-inch overlap. Fold the foil into thirds lengthwise. Lightly butter one side. With buttered side in, position foil around outside of dish; fasten with tape. Set aside.

Cook broken noodles in boiling salted water till *al dente*. Immediately drain in a colander. Rinse with cold water; drain. Set noodles aside.

Cook carrot and green onion in butter or margarine till tender but not brown. Stir in flour, salt, and nutmeg. Add cream or milk all at once. Cook and stir over medium heat till the mixture is thickened and bubbly. Cook and stir 1 minute more. Reduce heat to low. Add the Brie cheese and Parmesan cheese, stirring till the cheeses are melted. Remove from heat.

In a small mixing bowl beat egg yolks till thick and lemon colored. Slowly add the cheese mixture, stirring constantly. Fold the cooked noodles into the cheese-yolk mixture; cool slightly.

Using clean beaters beat egg whites in a large mixing bowl till stiff peaks form (tips stand straight). Gradually fold the cheese-yolk mixture into the beaten egg whites. Pour the mixture into the prepared soufflé dish. Bake in a 350° oven about 50 minutes or till a knife inserted near center comes out clean. Makes 3 main-dish servings.

EGGS AND CHEESE

For an elegant light supper, start with either the Brie Pasta Soufflé or the Cheddar Pasta Soufflé. Then add a few easy side dishes, such as a tossed salad, crusty bread, and your favorite wine. For dessert, serve whatever fresh fruit is in season and Gjetost cheese.

CHEDDAR PASTA SOUFFLE

⅛ recipe Onion Noodles, broken into ½-inch pieces (see recipes, pages 23 and 17)
2 tablespoons chopped onion
2 tablespoons butter *or* margarine
2 tablespoons all-purpose flour
  Dash pepper
1 cup light cream *or* milk
1 cup shredded cheddar cheese (4 ounces)
2 egg yolks
4 egg whites

Attach a foil collar to a 1-quart soufflé dish. For collar, measure enough foil to go around the dish plus a 2- to 3-inch overlap. Fold the foil into thirds lengthwise. Lightly butter one side. With buttered side in, position foil around outside of dish; fasten with tape. Set aside.

Cook broken noodles in boiling salted water till *al dente*. Immediately drain in a colander. Rinse with cold water; drain. Set noodles aside.

Cook onion in butter or margarine till tender but not brown. Stir in flour and pepper. Add cream or milk all at once. Cook and stir over medium heat till the mixture is thickened and bubbly. Cook and stir 1 minute more. Reduce heat to low. Add the shredded cheddar cheese, stirring till the cheese is melted. Remove from heat.

In a small mixing bowl beat egg yolks till thick and lemon colored. Slowly add the cheese mixture, stirring constantly. Fold the cooked noodles into the cheese-yolk mixture. Cool slightly.

Using clean beaters beat egg whites in a large mixing bowl till stiff peaks form (tips stand straight). Gradually fold the cheese-yolk mixture into the beaten egg whites. Pour into prepared soufflé dish. Bake in a 350° oven about 50 minutes or till a knife inserted near center comes out clean. Makes 3 main-dish servings.

GREEN AND WHITE LASAGNA

¼ recipe Spinach Lasagna Noodles
    (see recipes, pages 21 and 16) *or*
    ⅓ recipe Parsley Lasagna
    Noodles (see recipes, pages 23
    and 16)
1 slightly beaten egg
1½ cups ricotta cheese
⅛ teaspoon pepper
¾ pound broccoli, cut up, *or* one
    8-ounce package frozen chopped
    broccoli, thawed
¼ cup sliced green onion
3 tablespoons butter *or* margarine
2 tablespoons all-purpose flour
½ teaspoon dried dillweed
    Dash pepper
1 cup light cream *or* milk
1½ cups shredded process Swiss
    cheese (6 ounces)
½ cup grated Parmesan cheese

Cook lasagna noodles in boiling salted water till *al dente*; immediately drain. Rinse with cold water; drain. Set aside.

Stir together the beaten egg, ricotta cheese, and ⅛ teaspoon pepper. Set aside. If using fresh broccoli cook the broccoli in a small amount of boiling salted water about 5 minutes or till crisp-tender. If using frozen broccoli, cook according to package directions. Drain.

Cook onion in butter till tender but not brown. Stir in flour, dillweed, and dash pepper. Add light cream all at once. Cook and stir till bubbly. Cook and stir 1 minute more. Stir in Swiss cheese, stirring till cheese is melted. Stir broccoli into cheese mixture.

Arrange a single layer of lasagna noodles in the bottom of a greased 10x6x2-inch baking dish. Spread with *one-third* of the ricotta mixture, *one-third* of the cheese-broccoli mixture, and *one-third* of the Parmesan cheese. Repeat the layers of lasagna noodles, ricotta mixture, cheese-broccoli mixture, and Parmesan cheese two more times. Cover baking dish with foil. Bake in a 350° oven for 30 minutes. Uncover and bake for 5 to 10 minutes more or till heated through. Let stand 10 minutes before serving. Makes 6 main-dish servings.

EGG CONCHIGLIETTE CASSEROLE

4 ounces packaged conchigliette
    (small shells)
1 cup cubed fully cooked ham
1 cup sliced fresh mushrooms
¼ cup sliced green onion
1 clove garlic, minced
2 tablespoons butter *or* margarine
6 beaten eggs
⅓ cup milk
    Dash pepper
1 tablespoon butter *or* margarine
1 tablespoon all-purpose flour
    Dash pepper
¾ cup milk
½ cup shredded Monterey Jack
    cheese (2 ounces)
1 medium tomato, peeled, seeded,
    and chopped
¾ cup soft bread crumbs
2 tablespoons butter *or* margarine,
    melted
2 tablespoons grated Parmesan
    cheese
¼ teaspoon dried basil, crushed

Cook conchigliette in boiling salted water till *al dente*; drain. Rinse with cold water; drain. Meanwhile, in a skillet cook ham, mushrooms, onion, and garlic in 2 tablespoons butter till vegetables are tender. Beat together eggs, ⅓ cup milk, and dash pepper. Add to mixture in skillet. Cook without stirring till mixture begins to set on bottom and around edges. Lift and fold partially cooked eggs so uncooked portion flows underneath. Continue cooking and folding about 4 minutes more or till the egg mixture is cooked throughout but still glossy and moist. Remove from heat; set aside.

Melt 1 tablespoon butter or margarine. Stir in flour and dash pepper. Add ¾ cup milk all at once. Cook and stir till bubbly. Cook and stir 1 minute more. Stir in Monterey Jack cheese till melted. Gently stir together conchigliette, egg mixture, cheese mixture, and tomato. Turn into a greased 10x6x2-inch baking dish.

Toss together bread crumbs, 2 tablespoons melted butter or margarine, Parmesan cheese, and basil. Sprinkle atop egg mixture. Bake in a 350° oven for 15 to 20 minutes. Makes 6 main-dish servings.

ROTELLE AND CHEESY VEGETABLES

    4 ounces packaged rotelle
    2 cups coarsely shredded cabbage
    2 cups sliced carrots
    1 cup water
    1 medium onion, thinly sliced
    2 stalks celery, sliced
    ½ of a medium green pepper, chopped
    3 tablespoons butter *or* margarine
    3 tablespoons all-purpose flour
    2 teaspoons instant chicken bouillon granules
    1 cup shredded mozzarella cheese (4 ounces)
    1 cup shredded fontina cheese (4 ounces)
    ¼ cup grated Parmesan cheese
    ⅓ cup toasted wheat germ
    ¼ cup fine dry bread crumbs
    ¼ cup chopped walnuts
    2 tablespoons butter or margarine, melted

In a large saucepan cook rotelle in boiling salted water till *al dente*. Immediately drain in a colander. Rinse with cold water; drain. Set aside.

In the same saucepan cook cabbage and carrots in water about 10 minutes or till nearly tender. Drain well, reserving the liquid. Add enough water to reserved liquid to measure 1 cup total liquid. Set liquid and vegetables aside.

In same saucepan cook onion, celery, and green pepper in the 3 tablespoons butter or margarine till tender but not brown. Stir in the flour and bouillon granules. Add the reserved 1 cup liquid. Cook and stir till the mixture is thickened and bubbly. Cook and stir 1 minute more. Add the mozzarella cheese, fontina cheese, and Parmesan cheese, stirring till cheeses are melted. Gently stir in the rotelle, cabbage, and carrots.

Turn vegetable mixture into a greased 1½-quart casserole. Stir together the wheat germ, bread crumbs, walnuts, and the 2 tablespoons melted butter or margarine; sprinkle atop vegetable mixture. Bake in a 375° oven for 20 to 25 minutes or till hot and bubbly. Let stand 10 minutes. Makes 5 main-dish servings.

Three different sizes of shell pasta are available in supermarkets and pasta specialty shops. Conchiglioni refers to the pasta shaped like jumbo conch shells; conchiglie means the medium shells; and conchigliette are the tiny pasta shells.

CHEESE-STUFFED SHELLS WITH PARMESAN SAUCE

    16 packaged conchiglioni (jumbo shells)
    1 beaten egg
    ½ cup cream-style cottage cheese, drained
    ½ cup shredded mozzarella cheese (2 ounces)
    ¼ cup grated Parmesan cheese
    ¼ cup slivered almonds, toasted
    ¼ teaspoon dried dillweed
    ¼ teaspoon finely shredded lemon peel
    2 tablespoons butter *or* margarine
    2 tablespoons all-purpose flour
      Dash pepper
    1¼ cups milk
    ¼ cup grated Parmesan cheese
      Paprika

Cook conchiglioni in boiling salted water till *al dente*. Immediately drain in a colander. Rinse with cold water; drain. Set aside.

In a mixing bowl stir together beaten egg, cottage cheese, mozzarella cheese, ¼ cup Parmesan cheese, toasted almonds, dillweed, and lemon peel. Spoon cheese mixture into the cooked conchiglioni. Place the shells, filled side up, in a greased 12x7½x2-inch baking dish.

In a saucepan melt butter or margarine. Stir in the flour and pepper. Add the milk all at once. Cook and stir till the mixture is thickened and bubbly. Cook and stir 1 minute more. Stir in ¼ cup Parmesan cheese. Pour over filled conchiglioni. Sprinkle with paprika. Bake, covered, in a 350° oven for 20 to 25 minutes or till heated through. Makes 4 main-dish servings.

HERBED NOODLES AU GRATIN

¼ recipe Tomato Noodles (see recipes, pages 24 and 17) *or* ¼ recipe Spinach Noodles (see recipes, pages 21 and 17) *or* 8 ounces packaged medium spinach noodles
2 tablespoons butter *or* margarine
2 tablespoons all-purpose flour
1 teaspoon dried basil, crushed
½ teaspoon salt
  Dash pepper
2 cups milk
1 cup shredded mozzarella cheese (4 ounces)
1 cup shredded cheddar cheese (4 ounces)
1 large tomato, peeled, seeded, and chopped
½ cup soft bread crumbs
1 tablespoon butter *or* margarine, melted

Cook noodles in boiling salted water till *al dente.* Immediately drain in a colander. Rinse with cold water; drain. Set noodles aside.

In a saucepan melt the 2 tablespoons butter or margarine. Stir in flour, basil, salt, and pepper. Add milk all at once. Cook and stir till mixture is thickened and bubbly. Cook and stir 1 minute more. Add shredded mozzarella cheese and shredded cheddar cheese, stirring till melted. Fold in cooked noodles and chopped tomato. Spoon into 4 greased 10-ounce casseroles.

Toss together bread crumbs and the 1 tablespoon melted butter or margarine. Sprinkle some of the crumb mixture atop each casserole. Bake in a 350° oven about 20 minutes or till heated through. Makes 4 main-dish servings.

Au gratin is a French phrase meaning sprinkled with bread crumbs or shredded cheese and baked till brown. You'll find that Herbed Noodles Au Gratin certainly deserves the name, since it's flavored with both cheese and bread crumbs and is baked till it's a golden brown.

VEGETABLE-EGG BAKE

¼ recipe Whole Wheat Fettuccine (see recipes, pages 21 and 17) *or* 4 ounces packaged fettuccine *or* 4 ounces packaged spaghetti
1 10-ounce package frozen chopped broccoli
¼ cup chopped onion
1 clove garlic, minced
½ teaspoon crushed red pepper
1 tablespoon butter *or* margarine
1 cup grated Parmesan cheese
1 medium tomato, peeled and chopped
8 eggs

Cook fettuccine or spaghetti in boiling salted water till *al dente.* Immediately drain in a colander. Rinse with cold water; drain. Set aside.

Cook the frozen broccoli according to package directions. Drain well. In a saucepan cook chopped onion, minced garlic, and crushed red pepper in butter or margarine till onion is tender but not brown. Toss together cooked fettuccine or spaghetti, cooked broccoli, onion mixture, Parmesan cheese, and chopped tomato. Spoon fettuccine mixture into 4 greased 10-ounce casseroles.

Use the back of a spoon to make depressions in the fettuccine mixture in each casserole. Carefully break *two* eggs into the depression in *each* casserole. Sprinkle eggs lightly with salt and pepper. Bake in a 350° oven for 15 to 18 minutes or till the eggs are set. Makes 4 main-dish servings.

SPAGHETTI AND CHEESE PIE

8 ounces packaged spaghetti *or* 8
   ounces packaged fettuccine
½ pound bulk pork sausage
¼ cup chopped onion
¼ cup chopped green pepper
1½ cups shredded cheddar cheese
   (6 ounces)
2 tablespoons chopped pimiento
3 beaten eggs
1 cup milk
¼ teaspoon salt
   Dash pepper

Cook spaghetti or fettuccine in boiling salted water till *al dente*. Immediately drain in a colander. Rinse with cold water; drain. Set aside.

In a small skillet cook the bulk pork sausage, chopped onion, and chopped green pepper till the sausage is brown and the onion and green pepper are tender. Drain off fat.

Toss together cooked spaghetti or fettuccine, sausage mixture, the shredded cheddar cheese, and chopped pimiento. Turn mixture into a greased 12x7½x2-inch baking dish.

In a bowl stir together eggs, milk, salt, and pepper. Pour over spaghetti mixture in the baking dish. Bake, covered, in a 350° oven for 25 minutes. Uncover; bake about 15 minutes longer. Let stand for 10 minutes before serving. Cut into squares to serve. Makes 6 main-dish servings.

MEXICALI EGG MANICOTTI

10 Diable Manicotti (see recipes,
   pages 23 and 18)
8 beaten eggs
½ cup milk
1 4-ounce can mushroom stems and
   pieces, drained
1 4-ounce can green chili peppers,
   rinsed, seeded, and chopped
1 3-ounce package cream cheese,
   cut up
¼ teaspoon salt
   Dash pepper
2 tablespoons butter *or* margarine
1 15-ounce can tomato sauce
½ teaspoon chili powder
⅛ teaspoon garlic powder
¾ cup shredded Monterey Jack
   cheese (3 ounces)

Cook manicotti in boiling salted water till *al dente*. Immediately drain in a colander. Rinse with cold water; drain.

In a bowl beat together eggs, milk, mushrooms, *half* of the chili peppers, cream cheese, salt, and pepper. In a 10-inch skillet melt butter or margarine over medium heat. Pour in egg mixture. Cook, without stirring, till mixture begins to set on the bottom and around the edges. Lift and fold partially cooked eggs so the uncooked portion flows underneath. Continue cooking and folding about 4 minutes more or till egg mixture is cooked throughout but still glossy and moist. Remove from heat; set aside.

Fill each manicotti with some of the egg mixture according to the directions on page 18. Place in a greased 12x7½x2-inch baking dish. Stir together tomato sauce, chili powder, garlic powder, and remaining chili peppers. Spoon atop manicotti. Bake, covered, in a 350° oven about 10 minutes or till heated through. Sprinkle shredded Montery Jack cheese atop. Bake 5 minutes more or till cheese is melted. Makes 4 main-dish servings.

LAYERED CHEESE AND SPINACH

12 ounces packaged lasagna noodles
2 8-ounce packages cream cheese, softened
2 eggs
2 cups shredded provolone cheese (8 ounces)
½ cup cream-style cottage cheese
6 slices bacon, crisp-cooked, drained, and crumbled
⅛ teaspoon garlic powder
2 10-ounce packages frozen chopped spinach
½ cup sliced pitted ripe olives

Cook lasagna noodles in boiling salted water till *al dente*. Immediately drain in a colander. Rinse with cold water; drain. Set lasagna noodles aside.

In a large mixing bowl beat the cream cheese on medium speed of an electric mixer for 30 seconds. Add the eggs, beating till the mixture is fluffy. Stir in the shredded provolone cheese, cream-style cottage cheese, crumbled bacon, and garlic powder. Cook the frozen chopped spinach according to package directions; drain well.

Layer *half* of the lasagna noodles in a greased 13x9x2-inch baking dish. Spread with *half* the cheese mixture and *half* of the spinach. Top with the remaining lasagna noodles and remaining spinach. Stir olives into remaining cheese mixture; dollop across the top of the spinach. Cover and bake in a 350° oven about 30 minutes or till heated through. Makes 12 main-dish servings.

Scrambled Pasta and Eggs, a variation of the traditional scrambled eggs, makes an interesting main course for Sunday brunch. Try serving it with fruit juice or wine spritzers, sweet rolls, fruit salad, and coffee or tea.

SCRAMBLED PASTA AND EGGS

2 ounces packaged conchigliette (small shells)
4 beaten eggs
¼ cup milk
1 teaspoon prepared mustard
⅛ teaspoon salt
Dash pepper
3 slices bacon, crisp-cooked, drained, and crumbled
¼ cup shredded cheddar cheese (1 ounce)
1 tablespoon snipped parsley
2 tablespoons chopped green pepper
2 tablespoons butter *or* margarine

Cook conchigliette in boiling salted water till *al dente*. Immediately drain in a colander. Rinse with cold water; drain.

In a mixing bowl beat together eggs, milk, prepared mustard, salt, and pepper. Stir in conchigliette, crisp-cooked bacon, cheddar cheese, and snipped parsley. Set aside.

In an 8-inch skillet cook green pepper in butter or margarine till tender but not brown. Pour in egg mixture. Cook, without stirring, till the mixture begins to set on bottom and around edges. Using a large spoon or spatula, lift and fold the partially cooked egg mixture so the uncooked portion flows underneath. Continue cooking and folding about 4 minutes more or till the egg mixture is cooked throughout but still glossy and moist. Remove from heat and serve immediately. Makes 2 main-dish servings.

SURPRISE FRITTATA

¼ recipe Whole Wheat Fettuccine
(see recipes, pages 21 and 17) *or*
¼ recipe Herb Fettuccine (see
recipes, pages 22 and 17)
6 beaten eggs
¼ cup grated Romano cheese
¼ cup chopped onion
¼ cup light cream
1 tablespoon all-purpose flour
½ teaspoon dried oregano, crushed
¼ teaspoon salt
Dash pepper
1 cup shredded zucchini
1 cup shredded carrot
2 tablespoons butter *or* margarine
6 thin tomato slices (optional)

Cook fettuccine in boiling salted water till *al dente*. Immediately drain in a colander. Rinse with cold water; drain.

Stir together the eggs, Romano cheese, chopped onion, light cream, flour, oregano, salt, and pepper. Add fettuccine, tossing to coat. Set aside.

In a 10-inch oven-going skillet or omelet pan, cook zucchini and carrot in butter or margarine till tender but not brown. Evenly spread vegetables over bottom of skillet. Arrange tomato slices atop vegetables in skillet. Pour egg mixture over all.

Cook, without stirring, over medium-low heat about 8 minutes or till mixture begins to set around edges and bottom is lightly browned (surface will still be moist). As the eggs begin to set, run a spatula around the edge of the skillet, carefully lifting the mixture to allow the uncooked portion to flow underneath. Place the skillet or omelet pan under the broiler 4 to 5 inches from heat. Broil for 2 to 4 minutes or just till top is set. Loosen bottom of egg mixture and invert onto a serving platter. Garnish with additional tomato slices, if desired. Makes 4 main-dish servings.

EGGS AND CHEESE

Frittata is an Italian-style omelet that is cooked in the skillet and then broiled for a few minutes to give the eggs a slightly crusty edge.

CHEESE AND PASTA WEDGES

4 ounces packaged spaghetti
3 tablespoons sliced green onion
1 tablespoon butter *or* margarine
1 8-ounce can tomato sauce
2 tablespoons snipped parsley
¼ teaspoon dried thyme, crushed
2 beaten eggs
½ cup shredded mozzarella cheese
(2 ounces)
½ cup cream-style cottage cheese,
drained
¼ cup fine dry bread crumbs
¼ cup grated Parmesan cheese
3 tablespoons sliced green onion
½ teaspoon dried thyme, crushed
2 tablespoons butter *or* margarine

Cook the spaghetti in boiling salted water till *al dente*. Immediately drain in a colander. Rinse with cold water; drain.

For sauce cook 3 tablespoons green onion in the 1 tablespoon butter or margarine till tender but not brown. Stir in tomato sauce, parsley, and the ¼ teaspoon dried thyme. Bring to boiling; reduce heat. Cover and simmer about 10 minutes, stirring occasionally.

Meanwhile, stir together eggs, shredded mozzarella cheese, cottage cheese, bread crumbs, Parmesan cheese, 3 tablespoons green onion, and the ½ teaspoon dried thyme. Toss with spaghetti. In a heavy 10-inch skillet melt the 2 tablespoons butter or margarine. Spoon the spaghetti mixture into skillet, spreading evenly. Cook over medium-low heat about 10 minutes or till spaghetti mixture is golden brown on the bottom. Loosen spaghetti mixture with a spatula; transfer to serving platter. Cut into 4 wedges. Spoon sauce atop each wedge before serving. Makes 4 main-dish servings.

BROCCOLI-CHEESE PASTA RING

8 ounces packaged spaghetti
⅓ cup fine dry bread crumbs
1 cup shredded carrot
¼ cup sliced green onion
3 tablespoons butter *or* margarine
3 tablespoons all-purpose flour
½ teaspoon salt
½ teaspoon dried sage, crushed
⅛ teaspoon pepper
1½ cups milk
2 cups shredded cheddar cheese
2 beaten eggs
1 10-ounce package frozen chopped
    broccoli
2 tablespoons butter *or* margarine
2 tablespoons all-purpose flour
¼ teaspoon salt
1 cup milk
1 large tomato, peeled and chopped

Cook spaghetti in boiling salted water till *al dente*. Drain; set aside. Generously grease a 6½-cup ring mold. Sprinkle with bread crumbs. Set aside.

In a saucepan cook carrot and onion in 3 tablespoons butter till tender. Stir in 3 tablespoons flour, ½ teaspoon salt, sage, and ⅛ teaspoon pepper. Add the 1½ cups milk all at once. Cook and stir till bubbly; cook and stir 1 minute more. Add *1 cup* of the cheese, stirring till melted. Stir about *half* of the mixture into the eggs; return all to saucepan. Fold in spaghetti. Spoon into the prepared ring mold. Place mold in a larger pan. Pour hot water into the pan around the mold to a depth of 1 inch. Cover; bake in a 350° oven for 35 to 40 minutes or till a knife inserted near center comes out clean.

Remove mold from water. Let stand 5 minutes. Loosen mixture from mold by running a narrow metal spatula around both edges. Invert onto a serving platter.

Meanwhile, cook broccoli according to package directions; drain. Melt 2 tablespoons butter. Stir in 2 tablespoons flour, ¼ teaspoon salt, and dash *pepper*. Add the 1 cup milk. Cook and stir till bubbly; cook and stir 1 minute more. Stir in the remaining 1 cup cheese, broccoli, and tomato till cheese is melted. Serve broccoli-cheese mixture over spaghetti ring. Makes 6 main-dish servings.

If green rings form around the yolks of your eggs when you hard-cook them for the Layered Pasta Salad, don't worry. It is a harmless occurrence caused by the formation of iron sulfide. To lessen the possibility of such rings developing, place the eggs in a large saucepan and add enough water to cover the eggs. Bring water to a rapid boil over high heat. Reduce heat so the water is just below simmering and cook, covered, for 15 to 20 minutes. Immediately cool the eggs by immersing them in cold water. You might even want to add a few ice cubes to the cold water to speed the cooling.

LAYERED PASTA SALAD

6 ounces packaged cavatelli *or* 6
    ounces packaged anelli
4 cups torn fresh spinach
1 cup shredded cheddar cheese
    (4 ounces)
1 10-ounce package frozen peas,
    thawed
½ cup shelled pumpkin seeds,
    toasted
¼ cup sliced radishes
2 hard-cooked eggs, sliced
½ cup shredded carrot
2 cups torn lettuce
½ cup mayonnaise *or* salad dressing
1 3-ounce package cream cheese,
    softened
1 tablespoon milk
2 teaspoons lime juice
½ teaspoon salt
¼ teaspoon garlic powder
    Dash bottled hot pepper sauce
¼ cup shredded cheddar cheese
    (1 ounce)
2 tablespoons shelled pumpkin
    seeds, toasted

Cook cavatelli or anelli in boiling salted water till *al dente*. Immediately drain in a colander. Rinse with cold water; drain.

Place torn spinach in the bottom of a large salad bowl. In the following order, add the 1 cup shredded cheddar cheese, the cavatelli or anelli, *1¼ cups* of the peas, the ½ cup toasted pumpkin seeds, radishes, egg slices, shredded carrot, and torn lettuce.

In a blender container combine the remaining peas and the mayonnaise or salad dressing. Add the cream cheese, milk, lime juice, salt, garlic powder, and bottled hot pepper sauce. Cover; blend till the mixture is nearly smooth. Spoon over top of salad. Top with the ¼ cup cheese and the 2 tablespoons toasted pumpkin seeds. Toss to coat before serving. Makes 6 main-dish servings.

SPAGHETTI-WALNUT LOAF

8 ounces packaged spaghetti
1 cup shredded carrot
½ cup chopped onion
1 clove garlic, minced
2 tablespoons butter *or* margarine
¾ teaspoon dried thyme, crushed
½ teaspoon salt
Dash pepper
2 cups shredded mozzarella cheese
1 cup chopped walnuts
Toasted wheat germ
3 beaten eggs
¾ cup milk

Cook spaghetti in boiling salted water till *al dente*. Drain. Cook carrot, onion, and garlic in butter or margarine till tender. Stir in thyme, salt, and pepper. Toss together spaghetti, vegetable mixture, mozzarella cheese, and walnuts.

Lightly sprinkle a well-greased 9x5x3-inch loaf pan with wheat germ. Turn spaghetti mixture into pan. Stir together eggs and milk. Pour over spaghetti mixture. Bake in a 350° oven about 40 minutes or till firm. Let stand 10 minutes. Use a narrow metal spatula to loosen sides. Invert to remove from pan. To serve, cut into thick slices. Makes 6 main-dish servings.

FUSILLI A LA CARBONARA

10 ounces packaged fusilli *or* 10 ounces packaged spaghetti
3 slightly beaten eggs
⅔ cup grated Parmesan cheese
¼ cup snipped parsley
⅛ teaspoon white pepper
8 slices bacon, crisp-cooked, drained, and crumbled

Cook fusilli or spaghetti in boiling salted water till *al dente*. Immediately drain in a colander.

Meanwhile, in a bowl combine eggs, Parmesan cheese, parsley, and pepper. Toss hot fusilli or spaghetti with egg mixture. Sprinkle with crumbled bacon. Makes 4 main-dish servings.

CHEESY NUT-STUFFED PEPPERS

4 ounces packaged conchigliette (small shells)
4 large green peppers
½ cup chopped onion
1 clove garlic, minced
1 tablespoon butter *or* margarine
4 beaten eggs
2 cups shredded cheddar cheese (8 ounces)
1 cup broken walnuts
6 slices bacon, crisp-cooked, drained, and crumbled
½ teaspoon dried sage, crushed
¼ teaspoon salt

Cook conchigliette in boiling salted water till *al dente*. Immediately drain in a colander. Rinse with cold water; drain.

Cut tops from green peppers. Cut peppers in half lengthwise; discard seeds and membranes. Cook in boiling salted water for 3 to 5 minutes; invert to drain.

Cook onion and garlic in butter or margarine till tender but not brown. In a mixing bowl combine the beaten eggs, shredded cheese, walnuts, bacon, sage, salt, conchigliette, and onion mixture; mix well.

Season the green pepper shells with salt and pepper. Fill with conchigliette mixture. Place in a 13x9x2-inch baking dish. Bake, covered, in a 350° oven for 30 to 35 minutes or till done. Makes 8 main-dish servings.

LINGUINE WITH MUSHROOMS

2½ cups sliced fresh mushrooms
½ cup sliced green onion
3 tablespoons butter *or* margarine
½ cup dry white wine
¼ teaspoon salt
⅛ teaspoon pepper
⅓ cup whipping cream
½ recipe Basic Linguine (see recipes, pages 8 and 16) *or* 8 ounces packaged linguine

In a medium saucepan cook mushrooms and green onion in butter or margarine till tender but not brown. Stir in wine, salt, and pepper. Bring to boiling. Reduce heat; simmer, uncovered, for 25 to 30 minutes or till all liquid evaporates. Stir in cream; heat just till mixture becomes slightly thickened.

Meanwhile, cook linguine in boiling salted water till *al dente.* Immediately drain in a colander; turn linguine into a warm serving bowl. Pour mushroom mixture over linguine; toss till coated. Makes 8 side-dish servings.

PASTA WITH HERB BUTTER

⅓ recipe Onion Noodles (see recipes, pages 23 and 17)
3 tablespoons grated Parmesan cheese
3 tablespoons butter *or* margarine, melted
¼ teaspoon dried tarragon, crushed

Cook noodles in boiling salted water till *al dente.* Immediately drain in a colander. In a serving bowl toss together the hot noodles, Parmesan cheese, butter or margarine, and tarragon. Makes 6 side-dish servings.

MARINATED TOMATOES WITH PASTA

Pictured on the cover—

4 medium tomatoes, peeled and chopped
¼ cup snipped parsley
2 tablespoons olive oil *or* cooking oil
1 clove garlic, minced
1½ teaspoons dried basil, crushed
Dash pepper
½ recipe Basic Fettuccine (see recipes, pages 8 and 17) *or* 8 ounces packaged fettuccine

Toss together the chopped tomatoes, snipped parsley, olive oil or cooking oil, garlic, basil, and pepper; cover and refrigerate for 2 to 3 hours.

Cook fettuccine in boiling salted water till *al dente;* drain. Gently toss tomato mixture with fettuccine till well combined. Makes 8 side-dish servings.

PASTA VINAIGRETTE

¼ cup olive oil *or* cooking oil
¼ cup vinegar
1 small clove garlic, minced
1 tablespoon sugar
¾ teaspoon dry mustard
½ recipe Basic Linguine (see recipes, pages 8 and 16) *or* 8 ounces packaged linguine
½ cup sliced pimento-stuffed olives
½ cup sliced pitted ripe olives
2 tablespoon snipped parsley

For dressing, in a screw-top jar combine olive oil or cooking oil, vinegar, garlic, sugar, and mustard. Cover; shake well. Chill. Shake again before using.

Cook linguine in boiling salted water till *al dente.* Drain in a colander. Rinse with cold water; drain well. Toss dressing and olives with drained linguine till coated. Chill. Sprinkle with parsley before serving. Makes 8 side-dish servings.

Marinated Tomatoes With Pasta

BROCCOLI-CURRY PASTA TOSS

- 6 ounces packaged rigatoni *or* 6 ounces packaged mostaccioli *or* 6 ounces packaged cavatelli
- 2 cups broccoli buds *or* one 10-ounce package frozen cut broccoli
- ½ cup chopped onion
- 2 tablespoons butter *or* margarine
- 1½ to 2 teaspoons curry powder
- 2 tablespoons all-purpose flour
- ¼ teaspoon salt
- 1¼ cups milk
- ¼ cup peanuts

Cook rigatoni, mostaccioli, or cavatelli in boiling salted water till *al dente.* Immediately drain in a colander.

Meanwhile, cook fresh or frozen broccoli in a small amount of boiling salted water for 5 to 8 minutes or till crisp-tender. Drain and set aside.

For curry sauce in a small saucepan cook the chopped onion in the butter or margarine till tender but not brown. Stir in curry powder and cook for 1 minute. Stir in the flour and salt. Add the milk all at once. Cook and stir over medium heat till the mixture is thickened and bubbly. Cook and stir 1 minute more. Stir in cooked broccoli.

Toss the hot curry sauce with cooked rigatoni, mostaccioli, or cavatelli till the pasta is well coated. Sprinkle with peanuts just before serving. Makes 6 side-dish servings.

PASTA AND FAGIOLI

- 2 slices bacon
- 1 cup chopped onion
- ½ cup chopped green pepper
- 1 clove garlic, minced
- 1 16-ounce can tomatoes, cut up
- 1 bay leaf
- ½ teaspoon salt
- ½ teaspoon dried oregano, crushed
- ¼ teaspoon dried thyme, crushed
- ⅛ teaspoon pepper
- 1 15½-ounce can red kidney beans
- 4 ounces packaged farfalle *or* 4 ounces packaged elbow macaroni *or* 4 ounces packaged cavatelli
- Grated Parmesan cheese

In a large saucepan cook the bacon till crisp. Remove the bacon, reserving the drippings in saucepan. Crumble bacon; set aside.

Cook chopped onion, chopped green pepper, and minced garlic in reserved bacon drippings till the vegetables are tender but not brown. Stir in crumbled bacon, *undrained* tomatoes, bay leaf, salt, dried oregano, dried thyme, and pepper. Bring to boiling. Reduce heat and simmer, uncovered, for 5 minutes.

Stir in *undrained* kidney beans and *uncooked* farfalle, macaroni, or cavatelli. Bring mixture to boiling. Reduce heat; simmer, covered, for 10 to 13 minutes or till the pasta is *al dente*, stirring occasionally. Remove the bay leaf. Sprinkle with grated Parmesan cheese. Makes 8 side-dish servings.

CHILLED FETTUCCINE WITH CUCUMBER DRESSING

¼ recipe Whole Wheat Fettuccine (see recipes, pages 21 and 17) *or* 4 ounces packaged fettuccine
1 medium cucumber, seeded, shredded, and well drained
1 small onion, thinly sliced
¼ cup dairy sour cream
2 teaspoons sugar
2 teaspoons vinegar
¼ teaspoon salt

Cook fettuccine in boiling salted water till *al dente*. Immediately drain in a colander. Rinse with cold water; drain. Cover and chill for several hours. Stir together cucumber, onion, sour cream, sugar, vinegar, and salt. Cover and chill for several hours, stirring occasionally.

Place the chilled noodles on a large serving platter. Toss the cucumber mixture with the noodles till coated. Makes 6 side-dish servings.

FETTUCCINE ALFREDO

½ recipe Basic Fettuccine (see recipes, pages 8 and 17) or 8 ounces packaged fettuccine
2 tablespoons unsalted butter
½ cup light cream
½ cup grated Parmesan cheese
⅛ teaspoon white pepper
Ground nutmeg (optional)

Cook fettuccine in boiling salted water till *al dente*. Immediately drain in a colander. Meanwhile, in a saucepan melt butter over low heat. Stir in cream and heat through. Remove saucepan from heat. Add cooked fettuccine, Parmesan cheese, and white pepper to butter mixture, tossing gently till fettuccine is well coated. Transfer to a serving platter. Sprinkle with nutmeg, if desired. Makes 8 side-dish servings.

VEGETABLE GARDEN PRIMAVERA

½ recipe Basic Linguine (see recipes, pages 8 and 16) *or* 8 ounces packaged linguine *or* 8 ounces packaged spaghetti
2 medium yellow summer squash *or* zucchini, bias-sliced into ½-inch-thick pieces
2 cups broccoli buds
½ pound asparagus, bias-sliced into 1-inch-thick pieces
2 medium carrots, bias-sliced into ¼-inch-pieces
1 cup light cream
1 teaspoon dried basil, crushed
⅛ teaspoon pepper
2 ounces prosciutto *or* fully cooked ham, cut into thin strips
½ cup grated Parmesan cheese

Cook linguine or spaghetti in boiling salted water till *al dente*. Immediately drain in a colander.

Meanwhile, cook the yellow summer squash or zucchini, broccoli, asparagus, and carrots in a small amount of boiling salted water for 5 to 8 minutes or till vegetables are crisp-tender. Drain.

In a saucepan combine light cream, basil, and pepper; bring to a gentle boil. Boil for 8 to 10 minutes or till slightly thickened, stirring occasionally. Stir in prosciutto or ham. Toss together linguine or spaghetti, vegetable mixture, cream mixture, and grated Parmesan cheese. Makes 8 side-dish servings.

FAR EAST PRIMAVERA

½ cup cold water
¼ cup soy sauce
1 tablespoon sugar
1 tablespoon cornstarch
⅛ teaspoon crushed red pepper
⅓ recipe Whole Wheat Linguine (see recipes, pages 21 and 16) *or* 6 ounces packaged soba noodles (Japanese buckwheat noodles) *or* 6 ounces packaged spaghetti
2 teaspoons sesame oil
1 tablespoon cooking oil
1 tablespoon sesame seed
1 tablespoon sesame oil
¼ cup bias-sliced green onion
2 cloves garlic, minced
1 6-ounce package frozen pea pods, thawed
1 cup peeled lotus root, sliced crosswise *or* canned sliced lotus root
1 cup chopped bok choy
1 cup fresh bean sprouts
½ cup thinly sliced red *or* green sweet pepper

Combine water, soy sauce, sugar, cornstarch, and the crushed red pepper; set aside. Cook linguine or noodles in boiling salted water till *al dente.* Immediately drain in a colander. Toss with the 2 teaspoons sesame oil. Keep warm.

Preheat a large skillet or wok over high heat; add cooking oil. Cook sesame seed in cooking oil till lightly toasted. Add the 1 tablespoon sesame oil to skillet or wok. Stir-fry green onion and garlic in skillet or wok till onion is tender but not brown. Add pea pods, lotus root, bok choy, bean sprouts, and red or green sweet pepper. Stir-fry about 2 minutes or till vegetables are crisp-tender. Push vegetables to side of skillet or wok.

Stir soy sauce mixture; add to center of skillet or wok. Cook and stir till mixture is thickened and bubbly. Cook and stir 2 minutes more. Push vegetables into soy sauce mixture; cover and cook about 1 minute. To serve, twirl a portion of pasta onto a long-tined fork; push pasta off fork onto warm platter. Repeat with remaining pasta. (Or, turn pasta out onto warm platter.) Top with vegetable mixture. Makes 6 side-dish servings.

Lotus root is a common ingredient in oriental cooking. It is the root of a water lily that is somewhat like a potato and is used either alone as a vegetable or as part of a vegetable mixture. You can find fresh or canned lotus root in the specialty sections of your supermarket or in an Oriental food store.

RATATOUILLE AND FETTUCCINE

1 cup chopped onion
1 clove garlic, minced
2 tablespoons olive oil *or* cooking oil
1 16-ounce can tomatoes, cut up
1 8-ounce can tomato sauce
2 zucchini, cut into ½-inch slices
1 small eggplant, peeled and cubed
1 large green pepper, chopped
¼ cup snipped parsley
1 teaspoon dried oregano, crushed
½ teaspoon salt
⅛ teaspoon pepper
½ recipe Whole Wheat Fettuccine (see recipes, pages 21 and 17) *or* ¼ recipe Tomato Fettuccine (see recipes, pages 24 and 17) *or* 8 ounces packaged fettuccine

In a large saucepan cook chopped onion and minced garlic in olive oil or cooking oil till tender but not brown. Stir in *undrained* tomatoes, tomato sauce, sliced zucchini, cubed eggplant, chopped green pepper, snipped parsley, dried oregano, salt, and pepper.

Bring vegetable mixture to boiling; reduce heat. Simmer, covered, for 25 minutes. Uncover and cook for 5 to 10 minutes more or till of desired consistency.

Meanwhile, cook fettuccine in boiling salted water till *al dente.* Immediately drain in a colander. Serve vegetable mixture atop the hot cooked fettuccine. Makes 8 side-dish servings.

PASTA WITH SPICY HOT SAUCE

- 1 16-ounce can tomatoes, cut up
- 1 15-ounce can tomato sauce
- 1 4-ounce can green chili peppers, rinsed, seeded, and chopped
- 2 tablespoons snipped parsley
- 1 teaspoon sugar
- 1 teaspoon ground coriander
- ¼ teaspoon pepper
- 8 ounces packaged spaghetti
  Grated Parmesan cheese
  Crushed red pepper

In a 2-quart saucepan combine the *undrained* tomatoes, tomato sauce, chili peppers, parsley, sugar, coriander, and pepper. Bring to boiling. Reduce heat; simmer, uncovered, for 30 to 40 minutes or till desired consistency. Meanwhile, cook spaghetti in boiling salted water till *al dente*. Drain. Serve tomato mixture atop spaghetti. Pass Parmesan and red pepper. Makes 8 side-dish servings.

PASTA WITH SHRIMP SAUCE

- ⅛ recipe Spinach Linguine (see recipes, pages 21 and 16) *or* 4 ounces packaged linguine
- ½ cup sliced fresh mushrooms
- 1 tablespoon sliced green onion
- 1 tablespoon snipped parsley
- 1 tablespoon butter *or* margarine
- 1 tablespoon all-purpose flour
  Dash pepper
  Dash paprika
- ⅔ cup milk
- 1 4½-ounce can shrimp, rinsed and drained

Cook linguine in boiling salted water till *al dente*. Drain in a colander.

Meanwhile, for sauce cook the sliced mushrooms, onion, and parsley in butter or margarine till tender but not brown. Stir in flour, pepper, and paprika. Add milk all at once. Cook and stir till mixture is thickened and bubbly. Cook and stir 1 minute more. Stir in shrimp; cook and stir till heated through. Serve atop hot linguine. Makes 4 side-dish servings.

BEST TOMATOES

VEGETABLE NOODLE RING

- ¼ cup fine dry bread crumbs
- ½ recipe Onion Noodles (see recipes, pages 23 and 17)
- 1 cup coarsely shredded zucchini
- ½ cup chopped onion
- ½ cup chopped green pepper
- 3 tablespoons butter *or* margarine
- 3 tablespoons all-purpose flour
- ¾ teaspoon salt
- ⅛ teaspoon pepper
- 1½ cups milk
- 1 cup shredded Swiss cheese *or* cheddar cheese (4 ounces)
- 2 beaten eggs
- 1 10-ounce package frozen mixed vegetables
- 1 tablespoon butter *or* margarine

Generously grease a 6½-cup ring mold. Sprinkle with bread crumbs. Set aside. Cook noodles in boiling salted water till *al dente*. Immediately drain in a colander. Set aside.

In a large saucepan cook zucchini, chopped onion, and chopped green pepper in the 3 tablespoons butter or margarine till tender but not brown. Stir in flour, salt, and pepper. Add milk all at once. Cook and stir till mixture is thickened and bubbly. Cook and stir 1 minute more. Add shredded Swiss or cheddar cheese, stirring till cheese is melted.

Stir about *half* of the hot cheese mixture into beaten eggs; return all to saucepan. Fold in cooked noodles. Spoon into prepared ring mold. Place mold in a larger pan. Pour hot water into the pan around the mold to a depth of 1 inch. Cover; bake in a 350° oven for 35 to 40 minutes or till knife inserted near center comes out clean.

Remove mold from pan of water. Let stand 5 minutes. Loosen the noodle mixture by running a narrow metal spatula around both edges of the mold. Invert onto a serving platter.

Cook frozen vegetables according to package directions. Toss the vegetables with the 1 tablespoon butter or margarine. Fill center of ring with cooked vegetables. Makes 8 side-dish servings.

CAVATELLI AND THREE CHEESES

8 ounces packaged cavatelli *or*
   8 ounces packaged rotelle
2 tablespoons butter *or* margarine
2 tablespoons all-purpose flour
½ teaspoon salt
⅛ teaspoon ground nutmeg
   Dash pepper
2 cups milk
1 8-ounce package cream cheese,
   cut up
1 cup shredded mozzarella cheese
   (4 ounces)
¼ cup grated Parmesan cheese
1 medium tomato, sliced (optional)

Cook cavatelli or rotelle in boiling salted water till *al dente.* Immediately drain in a colander. Rinse with cold water; drain. Set aside.

For cheese sauce in a saucepan melt butter or margarine. Stir in flour, salt, nutmeg, and pepper. Add milk all at once. Cook and stir over medium heat till mixture is thickened and bubbly. Cook and stir 1 minute more. Stir in cut-up cream cheese and shredded mozzarella cheese till cheeses are melted.

Gently fold the cooked cavatelli or rotelle into the cheese sauce. Turn mixture into a greased 8x8x2-inch baking dish. Sprinkle with Parmesan cheese. Bake in a 350° oven about 30 minutes or till heated through. Garnish with sliced tomato, if desired. Makes 6 side-dish servings.

Timbales are traditionally custardlike dishes of chicken, fish, vegetables, or cheese that are prepared in molds or custard cups.

PEA AND PASTA TIMBALES

2 ounces packaged conchigliette
   (small shells)
2 slightly beaten eggs
1 cup light cream *or* milk
½ cup soft bread crumbs
2 tablespoons butter *or* margarine,
   melted
¼ teaspoon salt
¼ teaspoon ground nutmeg
1 cup frozen deluxe tiny peas,
   thawed
¼ cup shredded Swiss cheese
   (1 ounce)
2 tablespoons chopped pimiento
1 tablespoon finely chopped onion

Cook conchigliette in boiling salted water till *al dente.* Immediately drain in a colander. Rinse with cold water; drain.

Stir together eggs, light cream or milk, bread crumbs, melted butter or margarine, salt, and ground nutmeg. Fold in the drained conchigliette, peas, shredded Swiss cheese, chopped pimiento, and chopped onion. Pour mixture into six greased 6-ounce custard cups; place in a shallow pan. Pour hot water into the pan around custard cups to depth of 1 inch. Bake in a 350° oven for 30 to 35 minutes or till a knife inserted near the center comes out clean.

Remove the custard cups from the water. Let stand for 5 minutes. Loosen the mixture from the custard cups by running a narrow metal spatula around the edges. Invert the custard cups to unmold onto six serving plates. Makes 6 side-dish servings.

PASTA COLESLAW

    4 ounces packaged tripolini
        (about 1 cup)
    4 cups shredded red *or* green
        cabbage
    ½ cup shredded carrot
    2 tablespoons sliced green onion
    ¾ cup mayonnaise *or* salad dressing
    2 tablespoons vinegar
    2 teaspoons sugar
    ¾ teaspoon dry mustard
    ½ teaspoon salt
    ½ teaspoon celery seed

Cook tripolini in boiling salted water till *al dente*. Immediately drain in a colander. Rinse with cold water; drain.

In a large bowl combine tripolini, cabbage, carrot, and onion. Stir together mayonnaise or salad dressing, vinegar, sugar, dry mustard, salt, and celery seed. Pour over cabbage mixture; toss lightly to coat. Cover and chill for several hours. Makes 8 to 10 side-dish servings.

WILTED SPINACH AND PASTA

    6 ounces packaged rotelle
    8 cups torn spinach (about 10
        ounces)
    ¼ cup sliced green onion
    ¼ cup shredded carrot
        Pepper
    4 slices bacon, cut into 1-inch pieces
    1 tablespoon white wine vinegar
    1 tablespoon lemon juice
    ½ teaspoon sugar
    ¼ teaspoon salt
        Grated Parmesan cheese

Cook rotelle in boiling salted water till *al dente*. Immediately drain in a colander. Rinse with cold water; drain. Combine rotelle, spinach, green onion, and carrot. Sprinkle generously with pepper.

For dressing in a large skillet cook bacon till crisp. *Do not* drain off drippings. Stir in vinegar, lemon juice, sugar, and salt. Pour the dressing over the spinach mixture. Toss lightly to coat. Sprinkle with Parmesan cheese. Makes 6 side-dish servings.

When using fresh spinach, choose spinach with large, green leaves; avoid wilted or yellowed leaves. Before eating, rinse leaves in lukewarm water to remove sand. Remove and discard stems; pat dry with paper toweling. If you are storing the spinach for later use, keep the unwashed spinach loosely covered in the crisper section of your refrigerator.

DILLED FARFALLE SALAD

    ¼ recipe Basic Farfalle (see
        recipes, pages 8 and 17) *or* 4
        ounces packaged farfalle
    ½ cup shredded cheddar cheese
    ½ cup sliced celery
    ½ of a small green pepper, cut into
        1-inch strips
    2 tablespoons chopped pimiento
    ½ cup mayonnaise *or* salad dressing
    ½ teaspoon dried dillweed
    ¼ teaspoon salt

Cook farfalle in boiling salted water till *al dente*. Drain. Rinse with cold water; drain. Combine farfalle, cheese, celery, green pepper, and pimiento. Stir together mayonnaise, dillweed, salt, and dash *pepper;* pour over farfalle mixture. Toss lightly to coat. Cover; chill for several hours. If desired, serve in a lettuce-lined salad bowl. Makes 6 side-dish servings.

ORIENTAL TOSSED SALAD

    2 ounces rice sticks
        Cooking oil for deep-fat frying
    3 cups shredded cabbage
    1 8-ounce can sliced water chestnuts,
        drained
    1 cup fresh bean sprouts
    1 cup sliced fresh mushrooms
    1 6-ounce package frozen pea pods,
        thawed
    ⅓ cup salad oil
    ¼ cup vinegar
    1 tablespoon sugar
    1 tablespoon soy sauce
    ¼ teaspoon ground ginger

Fry *unsoaked* rice sticks, a few at a time, in deep hot cooking oil (375°) about 5 seconds or just till sticks puff and rise to top. Remove; drain on paper toweling.

Toss together rice sticks, cabbage, water chestnuts, bean sprouts, mushrooms, and pea pods. For dressing, in a screw-top jar combine salad oil, vinegar, sugar, soy sauce, and ginger. Cover; shake well. Pour over cabbage mixture. Toss lightly to coat. Makes 8 side-dish servings.

TORTELLINI SALAD

½ cup walnut halves
¼ cup pine nuts *or* slivered almonds
4 teaspoons olive oil *or* salad oil
½ cup ricotta cheese
2 tablespoons grated Parmesan cheese
1 teaspoon snipped fresh basil *or* ¼ teaspoon dried basil, crushed
Dash salt
Dash ground nutmeg
Dash pepper
1 recipe Basic Tortellini (see recipes, pages 8 and 13)
¼ cup olive oil *or* salad oil
3 tablespoons vinegar
½ teaspoon sugar
½ teaspoon snipped fresh basil *or* ⅛ teaspoon dried basil, crushed
¼ teaspoon salt
⅛ teaspoon pepper
Lettuce leaves

In a blender container combine walnuts and pine nuts or almonds. Cover; blend till finely chopped. With blender running on high speed, slowly add the 4 teaspoons olive oil or salad oil, blending till smooth. In a small mixing bowl beat ricotta cheese till smooth; add the nut mixture, the grated Parmesan cheese, the 1 teaspoon fresh basil, the dash salt, ground nutmeg, and the dash pepper. Beat till smooth and the consistency of soft butter. Fill tortellini with some of the ricotta mixture according to directions on page 13. Cook 8 ounces of the tortellini in boiling salted water till *al dente*. Drain. Rinse with cold water; drain. Cover; chill several hours. Store remaining filled tortellini according to the directions on page 8.

For the dressing, in a screw-top jar combine the ¼ cup salad oil or vegetable oil, vinegar, sugar, the ½ teaspoon fresh basil, the ¼ teaspoon salt, and the ⅛ teaspoon pepper. Cover; shake well to mix. Chill. Shake again just before serving. Serve the tortellini on individual lettuce-lined plates; drizzle with dressing. Makes 8 side-dish servings.

Miso paste, used in Rice-Stick Shrimp Salad, is a fermented soybean puree that is available at Oriental food markets. Use either a white or a red miso.
Also purchase five spice powder, which is a combination of cinnamon, pepper, aniseed, fennel, and cloves, at an Oriental market.

RICE STICK-SHRIMP SALAD

2 ounces rice sticks
Cooking oil *or* shortening for deep-fat frying
Spinach leaves
8 cups torn spinach (about 10 ounces)
1 8-ounce package frozen peeled and deveined shrimp, cooked, halved lengthwise, and chilled
1 medium zucchini, sliced and halved
½ cup sliced radishes
1 8-ounce can diced beets, chilled and drained
Miso Dressing

Fry *unsoaked* rice sticks, a few at a time, in deep hot cooking oil or shortening (375°) about 5 seconds or just till the sticks puff and rise to top. Remove with a slotted spoon; drain on paper toweling. Set aside.

Line a salad bowl with the spinach leaves. Place the 8 cups torn spinach in the bottom of the salad bowl. Place rice sticks atop spinach in center of bowl. Arrange a circle of shrimp around the rice sticks. Arrange a circle of zucchini and radishes around shrimp. Place a ring of beets around the zucchini-radish ring. Toss salad with Miso Dressing just before serving. Makes 6 side-dish servings.

Miso Dressing: In a screw-top jar combine 2 tablespoons *salad oil*, 2 tablespoons *rice vinegar or cider vinegar*, 2 tablespoons *water*, 1 tablespoon *miso paste or soy sauce*, ½ teaspoon *honey*, and ⅛ teaspoon *five spice powder*. Cover and shake well. Chill. Shake again just before serving.

CURRIED PASTA SALAD

2 medium carrots, sliced
1 medium turnip, peeled, halved, and thinly sliced
¼ recipe Basic Farfalle (see recipes, pages 8 and 17) *or* 4 ounces packaged farfalle
1 medium green pepper, cut into strips
¼ cup raisins
¼ cup vinegar
2 tablespoons sugar
2 tablespoons salad oil
1 teaspoon curry powder
¼ teaspoon salt
Dash pepper
½ cup peanuts
Romaine leaves

In a saucepan cook carrots and turnip, covered, in a small amount of boiling salted water about 5 minutes or till crisp-tender. Drain and cool. Meanwhile, cook farfalle in boiling salted water till *al dente*. Immediately drain in a colander. Rinse with cold water; drain. Toss together the carrot-turnip mixture, farfalle, green pepper, and raisins.

For dressing, in a screw-top jar combine vinegar, sugar, salad oil, curry powder, salt, and pepper. Cover and shake well. Pour over farfalle mixture. Toss lightly to coat. Cover and chill for several hours or overnight, stirring occasionally. Before serving, toss with peanuts. Serve in a romaine-lined salad bowl. Makes 4 side-dish servings.

Curried Pasta Salad

The fennel plant, native to southern Europe and the Mediterranean area, has been a flavorful favorite of cooks for centuries. The ancient Chinese, Indians, and Egyptians used fennel as a condiment; the Italians and Romans cooked it as a vegetable; and ancient Assyrian doctors mixed it in drugs. The seed of the fennel plant has the slight flavor of licorice.

AMBROSIA-STYLE PASTA SALAD

¼ recipe Orange Farfalle (see recipes, pages 24 and 17)
1 11-ounce can mandarin orange sections, drained
1 8-ounce can crushed pineapple (juice pack)
½ cup coconut
¾ cup dairy sour cream
⅛ teaspoon ground nutmeg

Cook farfalle in boiling salted water till *al dente*. Drain. Rinse with cold water; drain. In bowl combine farfalle, orange sections, *undrained* pineapple, and coconut. Combine sour cream and nutmeg; stir into fruit mixture. Cover; chill for 2 to 4 hours. Makes 6 side-dish servings.

BEAN AND SHELL SALAD

12 conchiglioni (jumbo shells)
1 17-ounce can three-bean salad
½ cup chopped cucumber
¼ cup chopped celery
¼ cup shredded carrot
2 tablespoons sliced green onion
2 tablespoons salad oil
½ teaspoon fennel seed, coarsely crushed
½ teaspoon dry mustard
Few drops bottled hot pepper sauce
3 cups shredded lettuce *or* cabbage

Cook conchiglioni in boiling salted water till *al dente*. Drain. Set aside.

Drain bean salad, reserving the liquid. Combine drained salad, cucumber, celery, carrot, and green onion. For the dressing combine reserved liquid, salad oil, fennel seed, dry mustard, and hot pepper sauce. Mix well. Stir *one-third* of the dressing into the vegetable mixture; toss lightly to coat. Spoon vegetable mixture into shells. Place shells in a shallow dish; pour remaining dressing over. Cover; chill for several hours. To serve, divide the shredded lettuce among 6 salad plates. Place 2 filled shells atop each. Makes 6 side-dish servings.

CREAMY ASPARAGUS PASTA SOUP

2 ounces packaged medium noodles
   (1½ cups)
½ cup chopped onion
1 tablespoon butter *or* margarine
2½ cups chicken broth
1 10-ounce package frozen cut
   asparagus
1 teaspoon lemon juice
⅛ teaspoon ground nutmeg
½ cup light cream *or* milk
   Snipped parsley (optional)

Cook noodles in boiling salted water till *al dente*. Drain. Set aside.

In a saucepan cook onion in butter or margarine till tender but not brown. Stir in broth, asparagus, lemon juice, and nutmeg. Bring to boiling. Reduce heat; cover and simmer for 5 to 8 minutes or till asparagus is tender.

Place *half* of the vegetable mixture and *half* of the cooked noodles in a blender container. Cover; blend till smooth. Remove to bowl. Repeat with remaining vegetable mixture and noodles. Return all to saucepan. Stir in cream or milk; heat through over low heat. Garnish with snipped parsley, if desired. Makes 6 to 8 side-dish servings.

ROMAN EGG SOUP

2 13¾-ounce cans chicken broth
2 ounces packaged acini di pepe
   (¼ cup)
1 slightly beaten egg
1 tablespoon lemon juice
2 teaspoons snipped parsley
   Dash pepper
   Grated Romano cheese

In a medium saucepan bring broth and acini di pepe to boiling. Reduce heat; simmer, covered, for 5 to 7 minutes or till acini di pepe is *al dente*.

Combine egg, lemon juice, parsley, and pepper. Pour gradually into the simmering broth, whipping gently with a wire whisk or fork till combined. Sprinkle with grated Romano cheese. Serve immediately. Makes 6 side-dish servings.

The use of sherry adds sophistication to this Mexican Vermicelli Soup. Another unusual aspect of the recipe is the sautéing of the uncooked noodles, which gives them a nutty taste.

Creamy Asparagus Pasta Soup makes a wonderful first course for a meal featuring veal or broiled chicken.

80

CHEESY SPINACH SOUP

½ cup chopped onion
1 clove garlic, minced
1 tablespoon butter *or* margarine
3 cups chicken broth
1 10-ounce package frozen chopped
   spinach, thawed and well
   drained
2 ounces packaged ditalini (½ cup)
3 cups milk
1 cup shredded cheddar cheese
⅛ teaspoon pepper

Cook onion and garlic in butter or margarine till tender. Add chicken broth; bring to boiling. Stir in spinach and ditalini; simmer about 7 minutes or till ditalini is *al dente*. Reduce heat; stir in milk, cheese, and pepper. Cook and stir over low heat till cheese is melted. *Do not boil.* Makes 8 side-dish servings.

MEXICAN VERMICELLI SOUP

1 tablespoon olive oil *or* cooking oil
1 ounce packaged vermicelli, broken
   into 2-inch pieces
½ cup chopped onion
1 10½-ounce can condensed beef
   broth
2 medium tomatoes, peeled, seeded,
   and chopped
1 cup water
   Dash ground red pepper
2 tablespoons dry sherry
1 tablespoon snipped parsley
2 tablespoons grated Parmesan
   cheese

In a saucepan over low heat, heat the olive oil or cooking oil. Add the *uncooked* vermicelli and cook till golden brown. Remove vermicelli; drain on paper toweling. Set aside.

Add onion to oil in saucepan and cook till tender. Stir in beef broth, tomatoes, water, red pepper, and browned vermicelli. Simmer, covered, about 15 minutes or till vermicelli is *al dente*. Stir in sherry and parsley. Sprinkle with Parmesan cheese. Makes 6 to 8 side-dish servings.

SHRIMP WONTON SOUP

1 4½-ounce can shrimp, rinsed, drained, and chopped
1 2-ounce can chopped mushrooms, drained
1 green onion, sliced
1½ teaspoons soy sauce
1 teaspoon grated gingerroot or ¼ teaspoon ground ginger
Dash pepper
24 Wonton Skins (see recipe, page 10) or 24 packaged wonton skins
4 cups chicken broth
2 teaspoons dry sherry
2 tablespoons snipped parsley

For filling, combine shrimp, mushrooms, onion, soy sauce, gingerroot or ground ginger, and pepper. Fill each wonton skin with some of the shrimp mixture according to the directions on page 10.

In a large saucepan combine the chicken broth and sherry; bring to boiling. Add filled wontons; return to boiling. Reduce heat; simmer, uncovered, for 6 minutes. Garnish with parsley. Makes 5 to 6 side-dish servings.

SPICY TOMATO SOUP

3 cups tomato juice
1 13¾-ounce can beef broth
1 bay leaf
2 teaspoons lemon juice
1 teaspoon Worcestershire sauce
⅛ teaspoon celery salt
⅛ teaspoon pepper
2 ounces packaged acini di pepe or 2 ounces packaged alphabet pasta (¼ cup)

In a saucepan combine tomato juice, beef broth, bay leaf, the lemon juice, Worcestershire sauce, celery salt, and pepper; bring to boiling. Add acini di pepe or alphabet pasta and cook over medium heat about 5 minutes or till acini di pepe is al dente. Remove bay leaf. Makes 6 side-dish servings.

Next time you prepare Vegetable Minestrone, try substituting a package of frozen succotash for the lima beans and whole kernel corn.

Pastina is the terminology used for all tiny pasta. Pastina comes in dozens of shapes, from miniature shells to stars, and usually appears in soup. In this book, we are calling for various pastinas by name, but you can easily substitute one for the other.

VEGETABLE MINESTRONE

½ cup chopped onion
½ cup chopped celery
1 small clove garlic, minced
1 tablespoon olive oil or cooking oil
2 cups water
1 16-ounce can tomatoes, cut up
1 medium potato, peeled and cubed (1 cup)
1 bay leaf
1 teaspoon dried basil, crushed
½ teaspoon salt
⅛ teaspoon ground sage
⅛ teaspoon pepper
1 8½-ounce can lima beans, drained
1 8½-ounce can whole kernel corn, drained
2 ounces packaged whole wheat medium noodles (1½ cups)
Grated Parmesan cheese (optional)

In a Dutch oven cook the onion, the celery, and the garlic in the olive oil or cooking oil till tender but not brown. Stir in the water, *undrained* tomatoes, cubed potato, bay leaf, dried basil, salt, ground sage, and pepper. Bring to boiling; reduce heat. Simmer, covered, for 15 minutes. Add lima beans and whole kernel corn. Bring to boiling; stir in noodles. Reduce heat; simmer, covered, about 10 minutes or till noodles are *al dente*. Remove bay leaf. Serve with the grated Parmesan cheese, if desired. Makes 8 side-dish servings.

CHICKEN LINGUINE SOUP

1   2½- to 3-pound broiler-fryer
      chicken, cut up
3   sprigs parsley
2   ¼-inch slices gingerroot
½   teaspoon salt
⅛   teaspoon pepper
¼   recipe Whole Wheat Linguine
      (see recipes, pages 21 and 16) *or* 4
      ounces packaged soba noodles
      (Japanese buckwheat noodles),
      broken up
2   tablespoons dry sherry
2   tablespoons soy sauce
1   6-ounce package frozen pea pods,
      thawed and bias-sliced
      lengthwise into 3 *or* 4 pieces
1   green onion, thinly sliced

In a large saucepan or Dutch oven combine chicken and enough *water* to cover (about 6 cups); add parsley, gingerroot, salt, and pepper. Cover; bring to boiling. Reduce heat; simmer about 1 hour or till chicken is tender. Remove the chicken; strain broth. Skim off excess fat. When chicken is cool enough to handle, remove and finely chop meat, discarding skin and bones.

  Measure the reserved chicken broth. Add enough *water,* if necessary, to equal 6 cups. Stir in linguine or soba noodles, sherry, and soy sauce; heat to boiling. Simmer, uncovered, about 8 minutes or till linguine or soba noodles are *al dente.* Stir in chopped chicken and pea pods; simmer, uncovered, for 1 to 2 minutes. Sprinkle with green onion. Makes 8 side-dish servings.

Italian Sausage Soup, served with a submarine sandwich, is a great warmer-upper to feed the gang after a cold night of sledding or skiing.

ITALIAN SAUSAGE SOUP

1   pound bulk Italian sausage
2   cloves garlic, minced
4   cups water
1   28-ounce can tomatoes, cut up
¾   cup dry red wine
2   tablespoons instant beef bouillon
      granules
1   teaspoon dried oregano, crushed
1   teaspoon Worcestershire sauce
½   teaspoon dried basil, crushed
1   9-ounce package frozen cut green
      beans
⅓   recipe Corn Farfalle (see recipes,
      pages 22 and 17) *or* 6 ounces
      packaged farfalle
4   stalks celery, bias-sliced into ½-
      inch slices
    Grated Parmesan cheese,
      (optional)

In a Dutch oven cook sausage and garlic till sausage is brown. Drain off fat. Stir in water, *undrained* tomatoes, red wine, beef bouillon granules, dried oregano, Worcestershire sauce, and dried basil. Bring the mixture to boiling. Reduce heat; cover and simmer for 30 minutes.

  Meanwhile, place the frozen green beans in a colander. Run hot water over the beans till separated. Stir the green beans, farfalle, and celery into the soup mixture. Return to boiling. Reduce heat and simmer, uncovered, for 10 to 15 minutes or till the farfalle is *al dente.* Sprinkle each serving with Parmesan cheese, if desired. Makes 6 side-dish servings.

WONTON COOKIES

½ cup chopped raisins
2 tablespoons brown sugar
2 tablespoons water
¼ cup chopped walnuts
1 tablespoon brandy
¼ teaspoon ground cinnamon
24 Wonton Skins (see recipe, page 10) *or* 24 packaged wonton skins
Cooking oil or shortening for deep-fat frying
Sifted powered sugar

For the filling, in a small saucepan combine chopped raisins, brown sugar, and water; bring to boiling. Cook, stirring constantly, over low heat about 3 minutes or till liquid is absorbed. Remove from heat; stir in walnuts, brandy, and cinnamon. Cool to room temperature.

Fill wonton skins with 1 teaspoon of the raisin filling. Position wonton skin with 1 point toward you. Fold bottom point of wonton skin over the raisin filling; tuck point under filling. Roll up wonton into a log. Wet point and press to seal. Wet inside of ends of each roll; twist ends to seal so that filling is completely enclosed. Repeat with the remaining wonton skins and filling. (For additional information, see how-to photos on pages 10 and 11.)

Fry filled wontons, a few at a time, in deep hot oil or shortening (365°) for 1 to 2 minutes or till golden brown. Drain on paper toweling. When cool, dust with sifted powdered sugar. Store in an airtight container. Makes 24 cookies.

SNACKS

You can often judge the size of pasta from its Italian suffix. For example, "oni" means large, as in conchiglioni. "Ini" means the pasta is small, as in stellini and tortellini.

PASTA CRISPS

1 recipe Lemon, Orange, *or* Pineapple Pasta (see recipes, pages 24 or 25)
Cooking oil for deep-fat frying
Sifted powdered sugar

Prepare desired pasta dough as directed. Divide dough into 6 balls. Place balls in a plastic bag and let rest 1 hour. On a lightly floured surface, roll out one ball at a time to ⅛-inch thickness. Cut each into 2x2-inch squares. Place the squares between layers of waxed paper till all 6 balls of dough are rolled out and cut.

Fry squares, 2 or 3 at a time, in deep hot cooking oil (375°) for 20 to 30 seconds or till lightly browned; turn once. Remove from hot oil; drain well. Dust with powdered sugar. Makes 6 dozen crisps.

SWEET SNACKS

8 ounces packaged fusilli, broken into 2-inch pieces
Cooking oil for deep-fat frying
1⅓ cups sugar
1 cup butter *or* margarine
½ cup light corn syrup
½ cup chopped pecans
1 teaspoon vanilla

Cook fusilli in boiling salted water till *al dente*. Drain. Pat dry. Fry cooked fusilli, about 12 pieces at a time, in deep hot oil (365°) for 1 to 2 minutes or till evenly browned; stir to separate. Drain. Repeat with remaining fusilli. Place in a buttered 13x9x2-inch baking pan.

Combine sugar, butter, and corn syrup. Cook and stir over medium heat till sugar dissolves and mixture comes to boiling. Cook, stirring occasionally, to 290° (soft-crack stage) and till syrup turns golden. Remove from heat; stir in nuts and vanilla. Quickly pour over fusilli. Mix well; turn out. Break up with forks. Store in a tightly covered container. Makes about 16 cups.

Deep Fried Stuffed Shells and Sweet Snacks

DEEP FRIED STUFFED SHELLS

Pictured on page 85—

- 16 packaged conchiglioni (jumbo shells)
- 1 beaten egg
- 1 6½-ounce can tuna, drained and flaked, *or* one 6-ounce can crab meat, drained, flaked, and cartilage removed
- 1 cup shredded cheddar cheese *or* Swiss cheese (4 ounces)
- 1 medium tomato, peeled, seeded, and chopped
- 2 tablespoons sliced green onion
- ½ teaspoon dried basil, crushed
- ⅛ teaspoon pepper
- 1 beaten egg
- 1 tablespoon water
- ⅔ cup fine dry bread crumbs
  Cooking oil *or* shortening for deep-fat frying
  Tartar sauce (optional)

Cook conchiglioni in boiling salted water till *al dente*. Immediately drain in a colander. Rinse with cold water; drain. Stir together the beaten egg, tuna or crab meat, cheddar or Swiss cheese, tomato, green onion, dried basil, and pepper. Stuff the cooked conchiglioni with the tuna or crab mixture.

Stir together the beaten egg and water. Dip each filled conchiglioni in the egg mixture and roll in bread crumbs. Fry in deep hot cooking oil or shortening (365°), a few at a time, for 1½ to 2 minutes or till golden brown. Drain on paper toweling. Serve conchiglioni with tartar sauce, if desired. Makes 16 appetizers.

CHICKEN EGG ROLLS

- 1 whole large chicken breast, skinned, halved lengthwise, and boned
- 1 tablespoon cooking oil
- 1 clove garlic, minced
- 1 16-ounce can bean sprouts, drained
- ½ cup chopped celery
- 2 tablespoons soy sauce
- 2 teaspoons cornstarch
- ½ teaspoon five spice powder
- 8 Egg Roll Skins (see recipe, page 10) *or* 8 packaged egg roll skins
  Cooking oil *or* shortening for deep-fat frying
  Plum Sauce

For filling, chop chicken. Preheat a large skillet or wok over high heat; add cooking oil. Stir-fry chopped chicken and minced garlic in the one tablespoon hot cooking oil for 2 minutes. Add the bean sprouts and the chopped celery; stir-fry about 2 minutes more. Stir together soy sauce and cornstarch. Stir in five spice powder. Stir into chicken mixture; cook and stir till thickened and bubbly. Cook and stir 2 minutes more. Cool to room temperature.

Place an egg roll skin with one point toward you. Spoon ¼ cup filling diagonally across and just below center of skin. Fold the bottom point of skin over the filling; tuck point under filling. Fold side corners over, forming an envelope shape. Roll up toward remaining corner; moisten point and press firmly to seal. Repeat with the remaining egg roll skins and filling.

Fry egg rolls, 2 or 3 at a time, in deep hot cooking oil or shortening (365°) for 2 to 3 minutes or till golden brown. Drain on paper toweling. Serve warm with Plum Sauce. Makes 8 egg rolls.

Plum Sauce: In a small saucepan combine ½ cup *plum preserves*, 1 tablespoon *vinegar*, 1 tablespoon *soy sauce*, ⅛ teaspoon *garlic powder*, ⅛ teaspoon *ground ginger*, and dash *ground red pepper*. Bring mixture to boiling, stirring constantly. Remove from heat; cool. Refrigerate in covered container overnight to blend seasonings.

BEEF EGG ROLLS

¾ pound ground beef
1 clove garlic, minced
1 8-ounce can bamboo shoots,
    finely chopped
½ cup chopped fresh mushrooms
¼ cup chopped green onion
2 teaspoons grated gingerroot
1 beaten egg
2 tablespoons dry red wine
8 Egg Roll Skins (see recipe, page 10)
    or 8 packaged egg roll skins
    Cooking oil or shortening for
      deep-fat frying
    Horseradish Sauce

In a skillet cook ground beef and garlic till meat is brown. Drain off fat. Stir in bamboo shoots, mushrooms, green onion, and grated gingerroot. Cook, uncovered, for 1 to 2 minutes. In a bowl combine the beef-vegetable mixture, egg, and wine; mix well.

Place an egg roll skin with one point toward you. Spoon ⅓ cup filling diagonally across and just below center of skin. Fold bottom point of skin over filling; tuck point under filling. Fold side corners over, forming envelope shape. Roll up toward remaining corner; moisten point and press firmly to seal. Repeat with remaining egg roll skins and filling.

Fry egg rolls, a few at a time, in deep hot cooking oil or shortening (365°) for 2 to 3 minutes or till golden brown. Drain on paper toweling. Serve warm with Horseradish Sauce. Makes 8 egg rolls.

Horseradish Sauce: Combine 3 tablespoons *chili sauce*, 2 tablespoons prepared *horseradish*, 1 tablespoon *catsup*, 2 teaspoons *lemon juice*, 2 teaspoons *soy sauce*, and ½ teaspoon *garlic powder;* mix well.

Gingerroot is a brown, gnarled root available in produce sections of supermarkets throughout the country. Because gingerroot will dehydrate easily, it is best stored in tightly sealed plastic storage bags or food containers. It will stay fresh for several weeks in the crisper drawer of your refrigerator.

CHINESE VEGETARIAN EGG ROLLS

1 tablespoon cooking oil
2 cups small spinach leaves
1 cup shredded carrot
1 cup chopped cabbage
1 cup chopped fresh mushrooms
½ cup thinly sliced green onion
½ cup chopped water chestnuts
½ cup chopped pea pods
½ cup chopped bamboo shoots
1 clove garlic, minced
1 teaspoon grated gingerroot
1 beaten egg
2 tablespoons soy sauce
1 tablespoon dry sherry
    Dash salt
12 Egg Roll Skins (see recipe, page 10)
    or 12 packaged egg roll skins
    Cooking oil for deep-fat frying
    Sweet and Sour Sauce

Preheat a large skillet or wok over high heat; add the one tablespoon cooking oil. Stir-fry spinach, carrot, cabbage, mushrooms, onion, water chestnuts, pea pods, bamboo shoots, garlic, and gingerroot for 2 to 3 minutes. In a bowl combine egg, soy sauce, sherry, and salt; stir in the vegetable mixture.

Place an egg roll skin with one point toward you. Spoon ¼ cup vegetable filling diagonally across and just below center of skin. Fold bottom point of the skin over the filling; tuck point under filling. Fold side corners over, forming an envelope shape. Roll up toward remaining corner, moisten point; press firmly to seal. Repeat with remaining egg roll skins and filling.

Fry egg rolls, a few at a time, in deep hot cooking oil (365°) for 2 to 3 minutes or till golden brown. Drain on paper toweling. Serve warm with Sweet and Sour Sauce. Makes 12 egg rolls.

Sweet and Sour Sauce: In a small saucepan stir together ½ cup packed *brown sugar* and 1 tablespoon *cornstarch.* Stir in ⅓ cup *red wine vinegar,* ⅓ cup *chicken broth,* ¼ cup finely chopped *green pepper,* 2 tablespoons chopped *pimiento,* 1 tablespoon *soy sauce,* ¼ teaspoon *garlic powder,* and ¼ teaspoon ground *ginger.* Cook and stir till bubbly.

TORTELLINI ROCKEFELLER

1 3¾-ounce can smoked oysters,
  finely chopped
1 tablespoon snipped parsley
⅛ teaspoon paprika
  Dash pepper
½ recipe Basic Tortellini (see recipes,
  pages 8 and 13)
  Spinach Sauce

For filling, combine chopped oysters, snipped parsley, paprika, and pepper. Fill tortellini with some of the oyster mixture according to directions on page 13. Cook tortellini in boiling salted water till *al dente*. Immediately drain in a colander. Serve hot or cold with Spinach Sauce. (If serving cold, rinse with cold water; drain. Cover and chill in refrigerator for 2 to 4 hours before serving).

Spinach Sauce: In a small saucepan combine 1½ cups finely torn and lightly packed *spinach leaves,* 2 tablespoons sliced *green onion,* and ¼ cup *water.* Bring to boiling. Reduce heat; cover and simmer for 1 minute. Drain, discarding liquid. In a blender container combine spinach-onion mixture, ¼ cup dairy *sour cream,* ¼ cup *mayonnaise or salad dressing,* 1 tablespoon *lemon juice,* and ⅛ teaspoon *dry mustard.* Cover and blend till smooth. Return mixture to saucepan. Cook and stir over low heat till heated through. *Do not boil.* Serve hot or cold with tortellini.

For a unique and elegant way to serve Tortellini Rockefeller at your next cocktail party, place the filled tortellini in half of an oyster shell and spoon the Spinach Sauce atop.

APPETIZER PASTA CROQUETTES

2 ounces conchigliette (tiny shells)
  (½ cup)
¼ cup finely chopped onion
3 tablespoons butter *or* margarine
3 tablespoons all-purpose flour
⅛ teaspoon pepper
¾ cup milk
2½ cups ground cooked chicken *or*
  turkey
1 2-ounce can mushroom stems and
  pieces, drained
2 tablespoons snipped parsley
1 beaten egg
2 tablespoons water
¾ cup Italian-seasoned fine dry bread
  crumbs
  Cooking oil *or* shortening for
  deep-fat frying
  Mustard Sauce

Cook the conchigliette in boiling salted water till *al dente.* Immediately drain in a colander.

Meanwhile, in a saucepan cook onion in butter or margarine till tender but not brown; stir in flour and pepper. Add milk all at once. Cook and stir till thickened and bubbly. Cook and stir 1 minute more. Remove from heat. Stir in chicken or turkey, mushrooms, parsley, and conchigliette. Cover and chill thoroughly. Shape cold chicken mixture into twenty-eight 1½-inch balls, using about 2 tablespoons mixture for each. Stir together egg and water. Dip ball in egg mixture; roll in bread crumbs. Fry the chicken balls, 2 or 3 at a time, in deep hot cooking oil or shortening (375°) for 1½ to 2 minutes or till golden brown. Remove with slotted spoon; drain on paper toweling. Serve warm with Mustard Sauce. Makes 28 appetizers.

Mustard Sauce: Combine 1 cup dairy *sour cream* and 1 tablespoon *Dijon-style mustard.* Stir in 1 to 2 tablespoons *milk* to make of dipping consistency.

SOUTH-OF-THE-BORDER WONTONS

¾ pound lean ground beef
⅓ cup chopped onion
1 clove garlic, minced
¼ cup canned green chili peppers, rinsed, seeded, and chopped
3 tablespoons tomato paste
¼ teaspoon ground cumin
48 Wonton Skins (see recipe, page 10) *or* 48 packaged wonton skins
Cooking oil *or* shortening for deep-fat frying
Frozen avocado dip, thawed (optional)
Taco sauce (optional)

For filling, cook beef, chopped onion, and minced garlic till meat is brown and onion is tender. Drain off fat. Stir in chopped chili peppers, tomato paste, and ground cumin. Fill each wonton skin with some of the beef filling according to the directions on page 10. (For additional information, see how-to photos on pages 10 and 11.)

Fry the wontons, a few at a time, in deep hot cooking oil or shortening (365°) for 2 to 3 minutes or till golden brown. Use a slotted spoon or wire strainer to remove the wontons. Drain on paper toweling. Serve the wontons warm with avocado dip or taco sauce, if desired. Makes 48 appetizers.

FETTUCCINE BACON QUICHE

Pastry for Single-Crust Pie
2 ounces Tomato Fettuccine (see recipes, pages 24 and 17) *or* Spinach Fettuccine (see recipes, pages 21 and 17) *or* 2 ounces packaged whole wheat fettuccine
1 cup shredded cheddar cheese
4 slices bacon
½ cup chopped onion
3 beaten eggs
1½ cups light cream
¼ teaspoon salt

Prepare Pastry for Single-Crust Pie. On a lightly floured surface flatten dough with hands. Roll dough from center to edge, forming a circle about 12 inches in diameter. Wrap pastry around rolling pin. Unroll onto a 9-inch pie plate. Ease pastry into pie plate, being careful not to stretch pastry. Trim to ½-inch beyond edge of pie plate; fold under extra pastry. Make a fluted, rope-shaped, or scalloped edge. To keep crust in shape, line the unpricked pastry shell with a double thickness of heavy-duty foil. Bake in a 450° oven for 5 minutes. Remove foil. Bake 5 to 7 minutes more or till pastry is nearly done. Remove from oven; cool. Reduce oven temperature to 325°.

Meanwhile, cook fettuccine in boiling salted water till *al dente*. Drain. Toss together fettuccine and cheese; place on bottom of cooled crust. Cook bacon till crisp; drain, reserving 1 tablespoon drippings. Crumble bacon; set aside. Cook onion in reserved drippings till tender; drain. Stir together eggs, cream, and salt. Stir in bacon and onion. Pour mixture into crust. Bake in a 325° oven for 30 to 35 minutes or till knife inserted near center comes out clean. Let stand 10 minutes. Makes 8 to 10 appetizer servings.

Pastry for Single-Crust Pie: In mixing bowl stir together 1¼ cups *all-purpose flour* and ½ teaspoon *salt*. Cut in ⅓ cup *shortening or lard* till pieces are size of small peas. Sprinkle 1 tablespoon *water* over part of the mixture; gently toss with a fork. Push to side of bowl. Repeat using 2 to 3 more tablespoons *water* till all is moistened. Form dough into a ball.

89

FRUIT-SAUCED LINGUINE

2 tablespoons cornstarch
1 tablespoon sugar
2 cups apricot nectar
2 inches stick cinnamon
2 whole cloves
3 cups peeled and sliced or cut up kiwis, cantaloupe, *or* peaches; sliced apple; raspberries; *or* halved strawberries
¼ cup dry white wine
⅓ recipe Orange Linguine (see recipes, pages 24 and 16) *or* ⅓ recipe Lemon Linguine (see recipes pages 25 and 16)

For sauce, in a large saucepan stir together cornstarch and sugar. Stir in the apricot nectar, cinnamon, and cloves. Cook and stir till bubbly. Reduce heat. Cover; simmer for 10 minutes, stirring occasionally. Strain to remove spices. Stir fruit and wine into sauce. Meanwhile, cook linguine in boiling salted water till *al dente*. Drain. Serve sauce atop linguine. Makes 8 dessert servings.

RAVIOLI WITH ORANGE SAUCE

2 3-ounce packages cream cheese, softened
1 egg yolk
2 tablespoons powdered sugar
¼ cup snipped dried apricots
½ recipe Orange Ravioli (see recipes, pages 24 and 14)
Orange Sauce

For filling, combine cream cheese and egg yolk. Stir in powdered sugar; mix well. Stir in apricots. Fill ravioli according to directions on pages 14 and 15. Cook ravioli in boiling salted water till *al dente*. Drain. Serve immediately with Orange Sauce. Makes 6 dessert servings.

Orange Sauce: Combine ¼ cup *sugar* and 1 tablespoon *cornstarch*. Stir in ¾ cup *orange juice*. Cook and stir till bubbly; continue 2 minutes more. Remove from heat; stir in 1 tablespoon *butter*.

Fruit-Sauced Linguine

ORANGE MERINGUE SQUARES

4 ounces packaged medium noodles
1 slightly beaten egg
½ cup chopped almonds, toasted
½ cup coconut
⅓ cup milk
¼ teaspoon ground nutmeg
3 egg yolks
1 cup dairy sour cream
1 package 6-serving-size *regular* vanilla pudding mix
1 cup milk
⅓ cup frozen orange juice concentrate, thawed
¼ teaspoon finely shredded orange peel (optional)
1 11-ounce can mandarin orange sections, drained
3 egg whites
½ teaspoon vanilla
¼ teaspoon cream of tartar
⅓ cup sugar

For crust cook noodles in boiling salted water till *al dente*. Immediately drain in a colander. Stir together the slightly beaten egg, chopped almonds, coconut, the ⅓ cup milk, nutmeg, and noodles. Turn into a greased 9x9x2-inch baking pan. Bake in a 350° oven about 10 minutes or till crust is set. Cool 10 minutes and then chill in the refrigerator for 20 minutes.

For filling in saucepan beat egg yolks slightly; add sour cream and vanilla pudding mix, stirring to mix well. Stir in the 1 cup milk, orange juice concentrate, and orange peel, if desired. Cook and stir till thickened and bubbly. Cool slightly. Stir in mandarin oranges. Pour mixture over cooled noodle crust.

For meringue beat egg whites, vanilla, and cream of tartar at medium speed of an electric mixer about 1 minute or till soft peaks form. Gradually add the ⅓ cup sugar, about 1 tablespoon at a time, beating at high speed about 4 minutes more or till mixture forms stiff, glossy peaks and sugar is dissolved. Immediately spread meringue over filling. Bake in a 350° oven for 12 to 15 minutes or till golden. Cool. Cover; chill to store. Makes 8 dessert servings.

NOODLE KUGEL

⅓ recipe Lemon Noodles (see recipes, pages 25 and 17) *or* 8 ounces packaged medium noodles
  2 tablespoons butter *or* margarine
  3 slightly beaten eggs
  2 cups dairy sour cream
  1 cup chopped, peeled apple
  ¾ cup light raisins
  ¾ cup milk
  ¼ cup sugar
  1 teaspoon ground cinnamon
  1 teaspoon vanilla
  1 tablespoon butter *or* margarine
  ¾ cup soft bread crumbs (1 slice)
      Dairy sour cream (optional)
      Strawberry preserves (optional)

In a large saucepan cook noodles in boiling salted water till *al dente*. Immediately drain in a colander. Return noodles to the saucepan and toss with the 2 tablespoons butter or margarine. In a large bowl stir together the slightly beaten eggs, sour cream, chopped apple, light raisins, milk, sugar, ground cinnamon, vanilla, and the cooked noodles. Turn mixture into a greased 12x7½x2-inch baking dish. Melt the 1 tablespoon butter or margarine; toss with the soft bread crumbs. Sprinkle atop mixture.

Bake in a 350° oven about 20 minutes or till the kugel is set. Serve the kugel warm or chilled with sour cream and strawberry preserves, if desired. Makes 8 dessert servings.

When Jewish cuisine established itself in the Middle Ages, vegetables were available only at harvest-time. As a result, kugels (puddings) were substituted for the vegetable course of a meal. Today, kugels are served sweet, salty, baked, or fried as a separate course, as an accompaniment to a meal, and occasionally as a dessert.

Flavor this elegant dessert, Caramel Pasta Flan, with Amaretto, an almond liqueur, or for an equally delicious dessert, substitute an orange liqueur or coffee-flavored liqueur for the Amaretto.

CARAMEL PASTA FLAN

2½ ounces packaged orzo or rosamarina, *or* 2½ ounces acini di pepe (about ⅓ cup)
  ½ cup sugar
  2 13-ounce cans (3⅓ cups) evaporated milk
  4 inches stick cinnamon, broken
  4 eggs
  ⅛ teaspoon salt
  ½ cup sugar
  ¼ cup Amaretto
      Sliced fresh strawberries (optional)
      Mint Sprig (optional)

Cook orzo, rosamarina, or acini di pepe in boiling salted water till *al dente*. Drain. To caramelize sugar, in a 10-skillet heat ½ cup sugar over medium heat, stirring constantly, till golden brown. Pour into an 8-inch flan pan or 8x1½-inch round baking dish; quickly tilt to coat bottom of pan. Sprinkle cooked orzo, rosamarina, or acini di pepe over caramelized sugar. In a saucepan heat evaporated milk and stick cinnamon till warm (110° to 115°); cool slightly. Discard cinnamon. Beat together eggs and salt; gradually add ½ cup sugar, beating well. Stir in the warm milk mixture and Amaretto. Carefully pour mixture into flan pan or baking dish. Set flan pan or baking dish in a larger baking pan on oven rack. Pour boiling water into the pan around the flan pan to a depth of 1-inch. Bake in a 325° oven for 45 to 50 minutes or till knife inserted near center comes out clean. (Center will be soft.) Chill. Invert onto a platter to serve. Garnish with sliced fresh strawberries and mint sprig, if desired. Makes 8 dessert servings.

Index

93

Tips